PALAZZO FARNESE

Sulla piazza omonima sorge il palazzo Farnese. L'architetto Antonio da Sangallo il Giovane ebbe l'ordine di costruzione dell'edificio dal Cardinale Alessandro Farnese (poi Paolo III) nel 1514. Viene chiamato « dado » dalla facciata del Sangallo, priva di fregi o di ricchi ornati e quindi quasi nuda come un « dado ». Il cornicione è di Michelangelo (1546) e la loggia, che si vede dalla via Giulia, è di Giacomo della Porta (1589).

Nell'interno, affreschi dei fratelli Carraci e del Domenichino.

LE PALAIS FARNESE

Le Palais Farnèse s'élève dans la place homonyme. L'ordre de construction du bâtiment fut donné à l'architecte Antoine da Sangallo le Jeune par le cardinal Alexandre Farnèse (devenu ensuite pape Paul III) en 1514. Il est appelé « le dé », sa façade, qui est l'oeuvre du Sangallo, étant dépourvue de frises et de riches ornements et pourtant presque nue comme un « dé ». La corniche est de Michel Ange (1546) et la loge, que l'on peut voir de la Voie Julienne, est de Giacomo della Porta (1589). Dans l'intérieur, fresque des frères Carraci et du Dominiquin.

THE FARNESE PALACE

The Farnese Palace rises on the homonymous square. Architect Antonio da Sangallo the Young was given the order to build it by Cardinal Alexander Farnese (who became pope Paul III later on) in 1514. It is called « the die » because of Sangallo's façade, which is devoid of friezes and rich ornaments and therefore is almost as bare as a « die ». The entablature is by Michael Angelo (1546) and the lodge, which can be seen from the Julian Way, is by Giacomo della Porta (1589). In the interior: frescoes by the Carraci Brothers and Domenichino.

DER FARNESE-PALAST

Am gleichnamigen Platze erhebt sich der Farnese-Palast. Der Baumeister Antonius da Sangallo der Junge empfing den Aufbaubefehl vom Kardinal Alexander Farnese (dann Pauli III) im Jahre 1514. Er wird « der Würfel » genannt, wegen der Vorderseite von Sangallo, die ohne Verzierungen und fast so nackt wie ein « Würfel » ist. Das Hauptgesims ist von Michelangelo (1546), und die Loge, die aus dem Julischen Wege zu sehen ist, ist von Giacomo della Porta (1589). Im Inneren: Fresken von den Gebrüdern Carraci und Domenichino.

PALACIO FARNESIO

En la plaza homónima se levanta el Palacio Farnesio. El cardénal Alejandro Farnesio (después Paulo III) ordenó la costrucción del palacio al arquitecto Antonio da Sangallo el Jóven en 1514. Es nombrado el « dado » por la fachada del Sangallo, que falta de frisos y ricos adornos y por eso está casi desnuda como un « dado ». El cornijón es de Miguel Angel (1546) y la galería, que se ve de la Vía Julia, es de Giacomo della Porta (1589). En el interior, frescos de los hermanos Carraci y del Dominiquino.

PALAZZO FARNESE

Vid torget med samma namn reser sig Farnesepalatset. På uppdrag av kardinal Alexander Farnese (sedermera Paulo III) fick arkitekt Antonio da Sangallo den yngre order att konstruera byggnaden. Den blev kallad « tärningen » på grund av Sangallo's fasad, som är utan ornamentering och sålunda nästan naken som en tärning. Taklisten är utförd av Michelangelo (1546) och loggian såsom den framkommer vid via Julia är utförd av Giacomo della Porta (1589).

I det inre finnas freskomålningar av bröderna Carraci och av Domenichino.

ESPRESSO
(EXPRÈS)

Mod. 24

Salute!

Food, Wine, & Travel in Southern Italy

Gail and Kevin Donovan and Simon Griffiths

with Robert Castellani

LAUREL
GLEN

Dedicated to:
Jeannie Donovan Fisher and Richard B. Fisher,
our friends and business partners, who made our
dream of Donovans come true
Our family and friends, for their endless support
The wonderful staff at Donovans, who make
the restaurant what it is
And Beau, our standard poodle

Laurel Glen Publishing
An imprint of the Advantage Publishers Group
5880 Oberlin Drive, San Diego, CA 92121-4794
www.advantagebooksonline.com

First published by Penguin Books Australia Ltd 2000

ISBN 1-57145-685-6

Library of Congress Cataloging-in-Publication Data

Donovan, Gail.
  Salute! : food, wine, & travel in Southern Italy / Gail and Kevin Donovan and Simon Griffiths, with Robert Castellani.
    p. cm.
  ISBN 1-57145-685-6
    1. Cookery, Italian–Southern style. 2. Italy–Description and travel. L Donovan, Kevin. II. Griffiths, Simon. III. Title.

TX723.2.S65 D66 2001
647.5945'7-dc21
2001035309

Designed by Danie Pout Design
Typeset in Stempel Garamond 10.5/15.5 pt by Post Pre-press, Brisbane
Americanization by TransAtlantic Chef
Printed in China by Midas Printing (Asia) Ltd

1 2 3 4 5   01 02 03 04 05

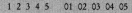

Contents

Acknowledgments

Julie Gibbs and Penguin Books Australia for their inspiration

Danie Pout, our graphic designer, for her dedication

Katie Purvis, our editor, for making us all look good

Darryl, Joseph, Sarah, and Donelle, for running the restaurant while we were away

Alec, Shane, Tannille, and Nina, for all their hard work on the recipes

Janet for babysitting Beau

Judy Gillard Travel

Dawn Caputo and Aida Firoiti at CIT Melbourne and Sydney

Dean Colton at Qantas

Pamela Pavitt at British Airways

Mary, Gianni, and Alessandro for lending us Robert for three weeks

Guru Val, for her guidance

Paula Poulson, our feng shui adviser

Miss Daisy at Empire III, Melbourne

Ron Hall and the gang at Supply & Demand, Melbourne

Barbara and staff at Market Imports, Melbourne

Andy Carlton at Tucker Seabrook for all the Campari

Christine Smith and Vicki Scott Murphy for all their typing

Frank and Andrew at Leeda Developments

Cathy Stonier Design

Mark at Camm Upholstery

John Portelli at Enoteca Silena–Di Santo, Melbourne

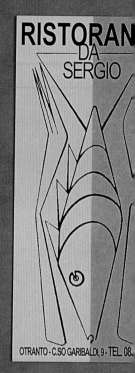

Foreword

I am proud to claim these four intrepid travelers as my friends. Robert Castellani was head chef at Stephanie's Restaurant for seven years, Simon Griffiths has shared adventures and taken beautiful photographs with me in Tuscany and in Australia, and over the years my friendship with Gail and Kevin Donovan has confirmed them as the most generous and professional colleagues one could ever know.

What a time they had together in southern Italy! It was travel as one hopes to experience it, with like-minded people, each bringing an individual interest to the shared adventure. The result is this totally delightful and inspirational book. It is a lively account of the hoped-for and the unexpected, with a satisfying mix of the sacred and the profane—put another way, there is plenty of serious information here about food, wine, history, and landscape, but serious attention is also given to shopping!

Gail has a clever and unerring eye for detail and style, be it people-watching, buying a linen shirt, or appreciating a view of Mount Etna by moonlight while sipping a Campari from a convenient terrace. It is her voice that leads us on this odyssey, and her commentary is vivid. We experience driving on the terrifying roads with the intrepid Kevin ("Fangio") at the wheel. We feel the heat of early summer and the violence of the sirocco winds, and can almost taste the gelato and the delicious breakfast pastries. Her reminiscences of the horror of Palermo's traffic echo my own recent experience.

Simon's lovely photographs capture beautifully the people, the places, and the food; these are images taken by someone whose heart has been engaged as much as his eye. (After all, as Gail says several times in the text, Simon wants to go and live in the south of Italy.) Kevin has contributed intelligent and approachable tasting notes that will encourage wine lovers to try the wines from the regions visited. And I love Robert's grave and unexpected utterances and historical notes.

When it comes to food, these four travelers are never fooled by the showy or the fashionable. The recipes they have selected include many classics, described in straightforward detail and all totally achievable by any interested cook. But there are also many lesser-known gems. I have marked the stuffed squid, a fava bean pasta sauce, and an orange and lemon breakfast cake as my first three to try.

In my own travels I have had the merest whiff of Sicily and want to return some day, but I would really like the Famous Four to come along too! Gail wonders if some of the traditional skills and activities they witnessed in southern Italy will be passed on to future generations. She hopes so, and so do I, but I tend to be more pessimistic than she is.

This book will inspire many readers to make a similar journey to the one described in these pages. My advice would be to go soon.

Stephanie Alexander

Introduction

Meet Gail and Kevin Donovan—Mr. and Mrs., to be exact. Partners in love, life, and the pursuit of running a successful restaurant.

We'd been talking for more than two years about going to Italy for a rest and some inspiration. During that time Donovans, our restaurant in the inner-city Melbourne bayside suburb of St. Kilda, had come to fruition in the old bathers' pavilion. We had dreamed of a restaurant that felt like home and dared to be different, and it was an instant success. Everyone asked how or where we got the idea. How did it evolve? The answer is a combination of our partners and friends, Dick and Jeannie in America; the years that Kevin and I had spent in the business; our amazing staff; and friends who had something to say about everything (and still have). Add several trips overseas—especially to the east coast of America, Kevin's home—and there it was.

We wanted Donovans to evolve continuously, and travel was a sure way to clear our minds and fill them with a stack of inspiring new ideas. Kevin had never been to Italy and I encouraged him to take an unusual journey from Rome south to Sicily, where I had lived long ago. Donovans needed a theme for summer. Perhaps cooking over the coals, such as the Italians do so well, could inspire a new facet of the restaurant—an additional functional area that at present was a storeroom of sorts. I wanted to see this kind of cooking first-hand.

We first met Simon Griffiths at our wedding in 1993. We ran the Melbourne restaurant Chinois in those days, and Simon had been sent by a magazine to take photographs of the celebration. His career has blossomed since then, and he now has a reputation for food photography that is second to none, enhanced by the very successful books he has worked on.

We kept in touch with Simon over the years and when Donovans opened it became his regular stop for coffee and a chat. Of course our planned trip became a topic of conversation. Simon had traveled through southern Italy before on a previous project and desperately wanted to go back—so why not go with us? We already knew he loved to shop, eat, and drink as much as we did. It was as simple as that. Together we chose May/June, just prior to the full tourist season in Italy and our most peaceful time at the restaurant.

Over a couple of fine wines one night, the idea of writing a book came up. Simon could take the photographs as we were going, and Kevin and I would write a journal full of information, personal stories, and inspirational ideas for design and decor for the restaurant. And, of course, food. We would include recipes for everything magical we ate.

Chef Robert Castellani was, and still is, instrumental in the success of Donovans. His knowledge of cooking and willingness to share it with the kitchen brigade is unique. He is quiet, organized, and always looking for new ideas; and also quite a historian as far as food goes. We invited him to come with us—his heritage is Italian (his mother was born in Salina, off the coast of Sicily, and his father comes from Pavia in northern Italy), he speaks the language, and he could help us eat. The addition of Robert would round off the team.

Four very different people, seeing, feeling, tasting, and thinking, traveling to more than sixty destinations in three short weeks. How would it work out? Read on.

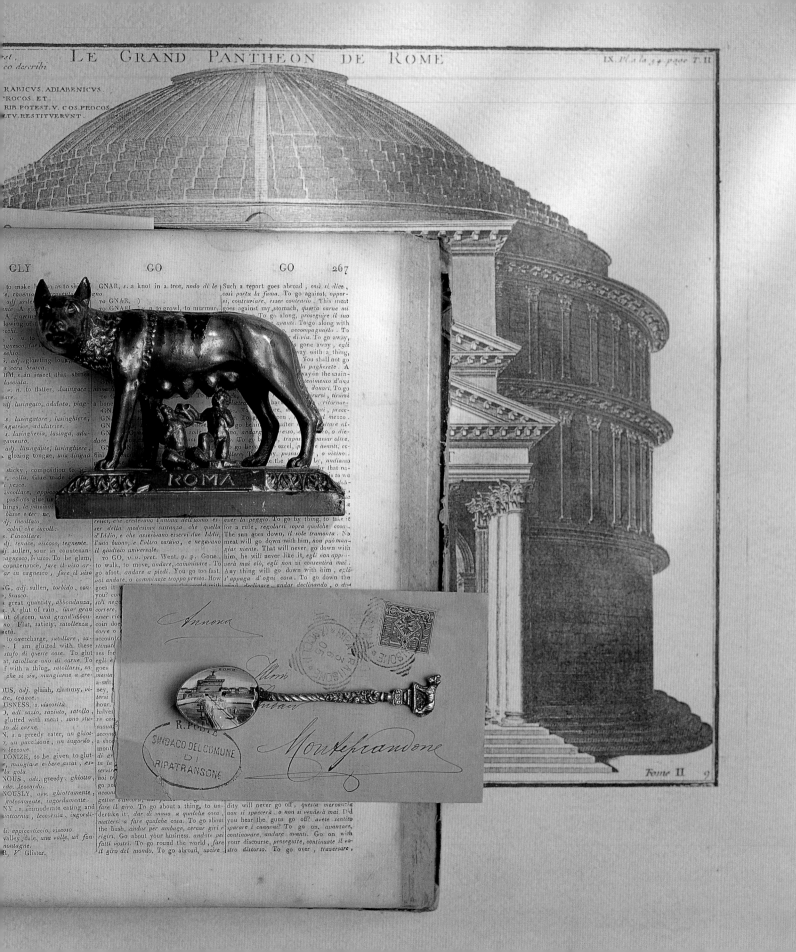

Rome Here We Come

Friday, May 21

After weeks of planning and 22 hours in transit, we see Sicily and southern Italy long before we land in Rome. "Hi, this is your captain. For those of you on the right-hand side of the plane, we are about to fly over Sicily and the view is crystal-clear."

What an amazing sight! We have all researched so hard prior to departing that we feel we know southern Italy from every angle without even being there. In the distance the looming black peak of Mt. Etna, Sicily's very active volcano, is blowing smoke, its head above the scattered clouds.

This first glimpse of Etna sends my mind racing back some twenty years: how young I was, how I fell in love with the land, the food, the people, how I've dreamed of returning and sharing my memories with Kevin, swimming at my favorite lido. I hope the south still holds the treasures I remember and that everyone will love them. So far the four of us are getting along beautifully, comparing notes, swapping ideas, constantly chatting. I wonder if it will last. The journey ahead is demanding, with long distances to cover, much driving, and many destinations way off the beaten track.

The southern shore of Sicily is immediately below us. The coastal towns merge into a big crocheted rug of sand, green and ocher, divided by craggy hills. Agrigento—those must be the ruins we see. Mazara del Vallo—we see dozens of fishing boats returning to port from the Mediterranean. All of us want a better view, and we continuously swap seats with maps in hand, trying to recognize some of our destinations.

We fly away from Sicily and head north over Sorrento on the Amalfi coast, before finally starting our descent into Rome. Simon, camera in hand, is snapping everything he sees. Back in the clouds momentarily, we relax again until the long journey ends with a smooth touchdown in Rome at 7:50 a.m. local time.

After a short walk through a couple of airport corridors we take an elevator to Roma Termini train station. The train is quicker, cheaper, and much more relaxing than a taxi, according to Simon. We put our luggage down on the platform, and Kevin votes himself ticket purchaser. No one knows how he will manage it—the only two Italian words he knows are *ciao* (hello/goodbye) and *tutti* (everyone). Nonetheless he returns within seconds, tickets in hand, grinning like a Cheshire cat at his achievement.

On the train Kevin reads about Rome, Simon takes shots of the bright-red poppies growing alongside the railway line, Robert snoozes, and I look around and

3

listen to other passengers to see how much of my lost Italian language I can remember.

Reality strikes as we disembark in Rome. It's a long, long walk from our platform to the taxi stand, and what a culture shock. Our taxi driver is happy to squeeze us all into his station wagon, but his tolerance ends the second he is behind the wheel. We zoom at breakneck speed around every corner, changing lanes as though other cars and motorbikes don't exist.

Slightly dazed, we arrive at Hotel Locarno. It's completely charming and perfectly located near the Piazza del Popolo, in the center of Rome. A couple of delicious caffè lattes later, our rooms are ready. We shower, unpack, and meet in the lobby by 11:00 a.m. Rome here we come!

Simon is the tour guide as he knows Rome very well. It's so long since I was here that I hardly remember the city, and it's been ten years since Robert was here. Kevin, equipped with his *ciao* and *tutti*, is ready for his first Italian experience.

There's only one thing to do when you have packed as lightly as we have: shop! We all need something to wear for dinner tonight. Simon and I, the experienced shoppers, organize the tour quickly and well. Off to the Pantheon, via a multitude of winding cobblestoned streets full of clothing stores, antique shops, butchers, cafes, and luscious-looking Italian people. They sure do have a way about them. My broken Italian seems to be getting us through shopping; hopefully it will continue to improve.

We won't always be able to rely on Robert, as we plan to separate much of the time in order to see more.

Our first Italian meal is lunch at Trattoria Armando al Pantheon. It's inexpensive and delicious, a good recommendation from Kevin's research. This is a real Roman trattoria, which loosely means a family-owned and -operated business with house specialities such as spaghetti alla carbonara and deep-fried zucchini flowers. We love this! Restaurant owners serving real food, and simply delicious. The antipasto is wonderful, as are all the pasta dishes and the hand-rolled grissini.

We stroll to Piazza Navona, which was once a stadium that held chariot races. It is now a place to people-watch and do coffee at Caffè Dolce Vita. The stunning piazza is lined with Baroque palaces and has three fountains, including the masterpiece by Bernini, Fontana dei Fiumi (Fountain of the Rivers), in the center. The place is full of artists drawing on-the-spot portraits of tourists. There is a wonderful atmosphere here, with tourists and locals, teenage schoolkids, businesspeople, and women shopping for dinner all moving around. It's like they're doing a big square dance together.

In the late afternoon we stroll back toward our hotel via the maze of small streets. How unbelievably beautiful it is—despite having constantly to dodge Vespas, motorbikes, and cars in the narrow passageways while we wander bug-eyed from shop to shop. I can't help thinking that the beauty of this place is that just meters above us are

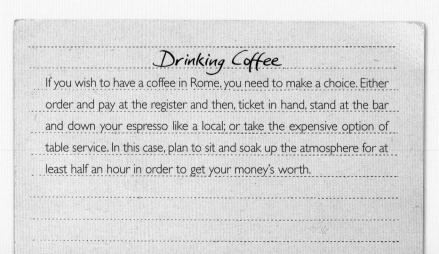

Drinking Coffee

If you wish to have a coffee in Rome, you need to make a choice. Either order and pay at the register and then, ticket in hand, stand at the bar and down your espresso like a local; or take the expensive option of table service. In this case, plan to sit and soak up the atmosphere for at least half an hour in order to get your money's worth.

Foyer of our hotel in Rome

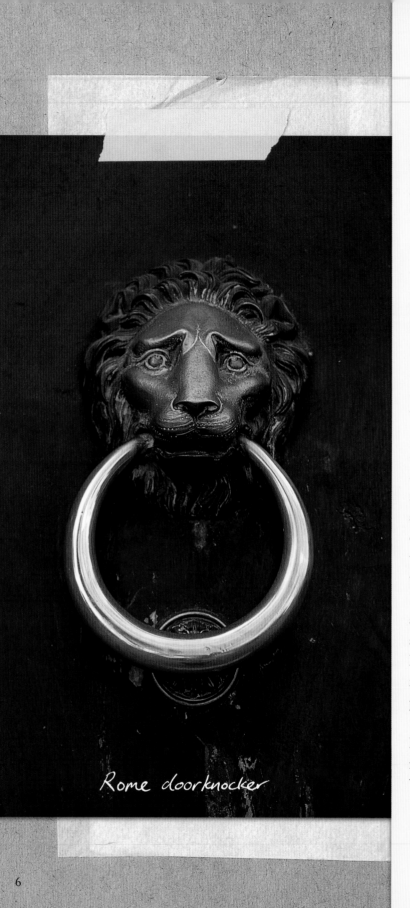

Rome doorknocker

countless apartments where people live, love, laugh, and eat. In so many places the treasured streetscapes, churches, and monuments would have ticket machines and fences around them. Here, they are a part of life. History, beauty, frescoes, graffiti, advertising, scaffolding, and beautiful people madly mixed together. It's the communities living and working in the heart of the city that make it magical.

Back at Hotel Locarno we sort through our purchases, then it's on with the new clothes and back out to dinner. Amazing—we are in Rome! We eat in a highly regarded restaurant in the medieval Jewish Ghetto. Ristorante Piperno, a bustling place with good food near Palazzo Cenci, is a twenty-minute taxi ride from Hotel Locarno. It's Friday night and the sound of Hebrew music and singing is everywhere. We eat the house specialities of fried artichokes, authentic Roman oxtail stew, and fresh fish, with good local wine.

However, for the first time (not the last, I imagine) we are treated as tourists. We experience none of the service style, finesse, or kindness that the locals around us are receiving. It's a good lesson for a restaurateur, to feel the anger that builds up when you are made to feel like you don't belong. If you spoke great Italian and could keep it up throughout dinner you could have a ball here. Unfortunately Robert can't cover up for all of us. Nevermind.

After the meal I have the day's worst idea. Refusing to ask the restaurant to call us a cab, I say, "We'll get one outside." The result is an hour-and-a-half's walk back to the hotel. If traveling in Rome, be sure to book your cab. Do not think of flagging a taxi in the street; they don't exist past 8:00 at night!

After 22 hours of traveling and a full day, no one will have trouble sleeping. Tomorrow we make an early start, for Saturday is market day. Before I close my eyes I hear the Vespas, sirens, and horns still buzzing outside. I'm in Italy.

Gail

Deep-fried Zucchini Flowers

Fritto di fiori di zucca

Serves 4

These are a favorite of the Roman antipasto table. As a variation, you can stuff the flowers with cheese and breadcrumbs.

¾ cup all-purpose flour
2 teaspoons extra-virgin olive oil
salt
¾–1 cup water
2 egg whites
extra olive oil for frying
21 ounces zucchini flowers, very fresh and still closed

1. Make a batter with flour, oil, salt, and water. It should be the consistency of cream. Set to rest for 1 hour.
2. Whip egg whites until stiff and fold into batter.
3. Heat extra olive oil in a skillet or frying pan. Dip flowers into batter and fry first on one side and then the other until nicely browned.
4. Drain on paper towels. Season to taste and serve piping-hot.

Spaghetti in the Style of the Coalminer

Spaghetti alla carbonara

Serves 4

This is a quintessential Roman pasta dish that has gained popularity all over the world due to the "friendliness" of its ingredients—pasta, eggs, and bacon. However, don't be tempted to substitute smoked bacon for the pancetta; the result will be inferior. Each person's serving should be liberally garnished with freshly ground black pepper in order to resemble the "dust" of the coalmine.

5 quarts water
4 tablespoons salt
¼ cup olive oil
5 ounces pancetta, diced
2 cloves garlic, crushed
2 large eggs
½ cup freshly grated Parmigiano-Reggiano
½ cup freshly grated pecorino romano
2 tablespoons cream (optional)
sea salt
freshly ground black pepper
1 pound good-quality spaghetti

1. Bring water and salt to a boil.
2. Meanwhile, heat olive oil in a saucepan, add pancetta and garlic and fry slowly over medium heat to remove fat from pancetta. Remove garlic from pan when browned.
3. While pancetta is rendering, combine eggs, half the cheese, cream, sea salt, and pepper in a bowl.
4. Cook spaghetti until al dente. Drain well but do not rinse.
5. Transfer spaghetti to a serving bowl and add pancetta, with its oil, and egg-cheese mixture. Toss with remaining cheese and adjust seasoning.
6. Finish with a generous amount of freshly ground pepper.

Oxtail in the Style of the Roman Butcher

Coda alla vaccinara

Serves 4–6

This dish typifies Roman cooking and is said to have its origins in the ancient stockyards of the city. The butchers of the Forum Boarium were given the hide, tail, and cheeks of the cattle as compensation for their labor. This dish does not require a vegetable accompaniment, but we enjoy it with a heaping spoonful of creamy mashed potato.

5½ pounds oxtail (about 4 oxtails), cut into 2 x 8 inch pieces
salt
freshly ground black pepper
all-purpose flour
½ cup extra-virgin olive oil
4 ounces pancetta, diced
3 cloves
3 small onions, halved
3 cloves garlic, minced
2 cups dry white wine *or* dry vermouth
28 ounces canned, peeled Italian tomatoes, with their juices
12 sticks celery, peeled of outer strings and cut into
   2-inch lengths
2 tablespoons pine nuts, toasted
2 tablespoons sultanas

1. Preheat oven to 350°F. Season oxtail and dredge in flour. Pat with your hands so that only a dusting of flour remains on oxtail.
2. In a large casserole with a lid, heat oil and fry pancetta until golden brown. Remove with a slotted spoon and reserve.
3. Brown oxtail thoroughly on all sides in pancetta oil. Do not crowd oxtail or allow pieces to touch during the process (brown in batches if necessary).
4. Return all oxtail to pan. Stick cloves into three of the onion halves and add to pan with remaining onion halves, reserved pancetta, and garlic. Reheat until sizzling.
5. Add wine and reduce until nearly evaporated. Add tomatoes and cover casserole tightly with aluminum foil. Cover with lid and bake until meat is very tender and falling off the bone, approximately 4 hours. Turn meat 2–3 times during cooking.
6. Add celery to casserole, ensuring it is covered with sauce, and bake for a further 20 minutes. Add pine nuts and sultanas. Continue baking until celery is tender, about 10 minutes.
7. Adjust seasoning and serve in a large bowl.

Note: This dish may be made 1 or 2 days in advance, stopping the cooking process before adding the celery. Allow to cool, cover, and refrigerate. Before serving time, remove any fat that has solidified on the surface. Rebubble on stove and continue with final 2 steps.

Rosemary and Chili Breadsticks

Grissini

Makes 50

Breadsticks are the main table decoration in every restaurant in Italy. They appear in brightly colored wrappers, waiting to be torn open and consumed to stop the rumbling of the stomach. Their production is so prolific that it seemed to us there were as many different brands as there were restaurants. This is the version we serve at Donovans. But be careful—they are very filling!

3¼ cups all-purpose flour
1½ teaspoons salt
2 teaspoons instant dried yeast
1 tablespoon dried chili flakes
½ cup freshly chopped rosemary
1 tablespoon sugar, honey, *or* malt syrup
2 tablespoons extra-virgin olive oil
1⅓ cups warm water
extra water
sea salt

1. In a mixing bowl, combine flour, salt, yeast, chili flakes, and rosemary. (Note: it is not necessary to allow instant yeast to "sponge" as you would with fresh yeast.)
2. Stir sugar and olive oil into warm water and mix into dry ingredients. Combine with your fingertips until a rough dough is formed. Remove dough from bowl and transfer to a lightly floured work surface. Knead gently until smooth, about 5 minutes.
3. Transfer to a lightly greased bowl and cover with a damp tea towel. Place in a warm, draft-free spot and allow dough to double in size, about 45 minutes.
4. Preheat oven to 350°F Lightly oil 2 cookie sheets.
5. Turn dough back onto work surface and knock down to its original size. Divide in half. Roll each half into a 4 x 12 inch rectangular sheet.
6. With a knife or pastry cutter, cut ½-inch strips from the short side of the first sheet. When all dough is cut, roll each strip on the work surface with the palm of your hand until an even strand of approximately 8 inches is formed. Transfer strands to cookie sheet. Repeat process with second sheet of dough.
7. Sprinkle breadsticks with a little water and sea salt. Bake for approximately 15 minutes or until golden brown and crisp.

Variation
Substitute ½ cup finely chopped green and black olives and ½ cup freshly grated Parmigiano-Reggiano for the rosemary and chili flakes, and use 1 cup warm water instead of 1⅓ cups.

Fried Artichokes, Jewish-style

Carciofi alla Giudea

Serves 4

4 cups water
juice of 1 lemon
8 medium-sized artichokes
olive oil
salt
freshly ground black pepper

1. Place water in a large bowl and add lemon juice. Trim each artichoke by removing the tough outer leaves and cutting off the stem. Remove tips of leaves with a sharp knife and drop artichoke into acidulated water while you trim the next artichoke. Drain trimmed artichokes and pat dry.

2. Crush artichokes gently, head down, with the back of your hand to loosen leaves and force artichokes to open slightly, resembling flowers.

3. Heat a liberal amount of olive oil in a saucepan. Place artichokes in oil, stem up. Brown evenly, turning as required.

4. Return artichokes to stem-up position. Press down on stems with a fork so that leaves spread open. Continue to cook until artichoke hearts are tender.

5. Drain on paper towels. Season with salt and pepper and serve immediately.

Highlights of the Day

Gail

Kevin

Simon

Robert

Smells

Rome has a smell—I got it the minute we were off the train and into the street. It is of motorbikes, coffee, restaurants, food, roasted chestnuts, and a touch of sweetness, and has the ability to transport me back in time to my last visit, some twenty years ago. I felt younger already. Bella Roma!

Arrival in Rome

Whenever I travel to a foreign country, I always have a feeling of trepidation when alighting. Is my passport in order? Will a secret button be pressed and will I be whisked off to a hidden room for interrogation? Not so in Italy. The young, attractive customs woman barely gave my passport a cursory glance. It seemed as though my three-month tourist visa had no starting point.

Poppies

Red streaks flashed past as we looked out the train windows heading into Rome from Fiumicino airport. The poppies were out and seemed to make the journey incredibly beautiful even though we were hurtling through suburbs of tower blocks and industry.

The Origins of Coffee

Ethiopia is thought to be the motherland of coffee beans—which found their way to Brazil and Colombia, the two largest coffee producers of today. Brewed coffee was first reserved for the medical profession as a digestive, and for the priesthood, who would use coffee to keep them awake through the long nights of religious practice. It's still a religion in Rome!

Roma - 138 - Foro Romano -
Tempio di Castore e Polluce

Coffee, Campari, & Colosseum

Saturday, May 22

Everyone looks much fresher today and is on the ball by 7:30 a.m. When you travel from one end of the earth to the other, it seems natural to wake-up early for the first few days.

We arrange a cab to Testaccio market, but the taxi driver insists it is only open on Sunday and our guidebook is incorrect. We opt for the smaller market at Campo de' Fiori. Later we find out the driver was lazy and just didn't want to head in the Testaccio direction.

It is our good fortune that we missed the bigger market, for Campo de' Fiori is completely gorgeous; a local market with very few tourists except for us. We spread out immediately. Kevin and I head for a little bar for coffee. Simon is taking photos as usual, and Robert is transfixed by the porcini mushroom stand, chatting to the stallholder for over an hour.

After our coffee, it's time to purchase food for a picnic lunch. Somehow my combination of mime, mixed words, total lack of correct grammar, and bits of English get us what we need: Parma ham, chili-marinated olives, pecorino romano cheese, and *bresaola*, delicious smoked beef. L'Antica Norcineria, famous for utilizing pigs from Norcia in the region of Umbria, makes the best sausages, prosciutto, pancetta, baked hams, and bacons in Rome, all in

their shop on the edge of the Campo market. To round off the menu for lunch we purchase bread from one of Rome's best bakeries, Forno di Campo de' Fiori, situated in another shop in the buildings around the market.

Back to the market stalls. The mixed salad greens, fresh artichokes of varied colors, oranges, berries, and mushrooms are breathtaking. The quaint little seafood stalls are full of rare sights: huge slabs of swordfish cut to order, clams, baby calamari, sole, sea bass, and red mullet. We recognize many of the varieties, but there are no words to translate all of them. I'd eat every different one; they are glistening with freshness.

Next, we're off to the Colosseum. In the small streets on the way to Nero's place, we discover some very inexpensive menswear stores with all the designer names, plus "The Fans" official football shop. I wind up looking like I could be the goalkeeper for Lazio. We are now carrying three bags of food for lunch, countless bags of clothes, presents we purchased in the market, and Simon's cameras. What a total lack of planning!

We round the corner from our shopping expedition and there it all is—one incredible piece of history after another. Facing us are the Palazzo dei Senatori and countless other amazing buildings. We climb the stairs to Piazza del Campidoglio, a Michelangelo-designed piazza famous for its geometric paving and building design. There are so many brides scattered over the paving having their album shots taken that we can hardly see the pattern. They are wearing every style of dress, from minimalist chic to what can only be described as a Mardi Gras float with a person inside it. We laugh a lot. Later we find out that it is wedding season in Rome.

Onward to the Forum, the center of ancient Roman political life. We completely fall in love with this place, sitting on collapsed piles of ruins, talking, and reading our guidebooks. It still has incredible power after all this time.

We pass the statue of the She-Wolf, the creature supposedly responsible for bringing up Romulus and Remus around the fifth century B.C. Cute myth and enchanting statue. I start fretting for Beau, our beautiful dog waiting at home in Australia. I also think of our wonderful staff at Donovans and assume they are in perfect control of the restaurant without us. Much too far away to worry now.

Next stop is Palazzo dei Conservatori and the Colosseum. It is breathtaking, but as wary travelers we see the signs of danger. It's crowded, full of in-your-face vendors, gangs of gypsy kids, and shady characters. We decide not to wait in the line, instead wandering to the park opposite to eat the delicious things we purchased at the market. Even then the vendors and shady characters follow us, and a good lunch is spoiled. Relieved to get away, we take a cab back to the hotel to drop off our bags, freshen up, and go again.

Just around the corner from our hotel Kevin discovers Buccone, a beautiful wine shop in the old section of Rome. It has a great wine collection and helpful owners. Kevin buys several bottles, which we use for a very special wine-tasting later in our room. He chose well!

Then Simon discovers, among the design and antique shops, the most unusual, ridiculous thing: a huge pewter wine bucket with lion's feet. We always purchase a special present for our restaurant wherever we go. This is absolutely it—I can tell by the look on Kevin's face. "Operating equipment," he says, which means that's how he will explain the expensive purchase to our accountant. Worse than the price is how heavy the thing is. We certainly can't carry it. It has to be sent home now.

Back to the hotel for a Campari and soda at the bar, then out to some of the hip places the hotel owner, Caterina Valente, has suggested. We head back in the direction of Campo de' Fiori to check out various bars and trattorias, choosing to eat with the locals at Cul de Sac wine bar. I can still taste the creamy *baccalà* (salt cod) and wonderful *cotechino* sausages. Full, tired, and home to sleep.

Gail

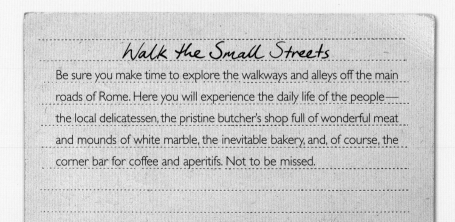

Walk the Small Streets

Be sure you make time to explore the walkways and alleys off the main roads of Rome. Here you will experience the daily life of the people— the local delicatessen, the pristine butcher's shop full of wonderful meat and mounds of white marble, the inevitable bakery, and, of course, the corner bar for coffee and aperitifs. Not to be missed.

Campo de' Fiori market

Pork Sausage with Lentils and Mustard Fruits

Cotechino con lenticchie e mostarda di Cremona

Serves 4–5

Cotechino is a traditional style of sausage made with pork rind, lean pork meat, and back fat. The coarse mixture is seasoned with cloves and cinnamon and formed in a pig casing. It usually weighs between 1 and 2 pounds, and measures 2–3 inches in diameter and 8 inches in length. The version we enjoyed in Rome was homemade, but we recommend you purchase yours from a good Italian butcher. One of cotechino's traditional accompaniments is mostarda di Cremona. This preserve, available from good Italian delicatessens, is a blend of various fruits that are candied and held in a thick syrup of honey and white wine and highly seasoned with spices and mustard, giving a sweet, hot piquancy.

1 fresh cotechino sausage
2½ cups brown lentils
¼ cup olive oil
1 onion, minced
1 stick celery, finely chopped
1 bay leaf
1 sprig thyme
butter
salt
freshly ground black pepper
1 cup mostarda di Cremona

1. Prick the sausage with a needle or fine skewer. Lay in a shallow pan and cover with cold water. Bring to a boil and reduce to a simmer. Cook sausage according to its weight, allowing 45 minutes for each pound.
2. While sausage is cooking, rinse and drain lentils. In a saucepan, heat olive oil and fry onion and celery until translucent. Add lentils, bay leaf, and thyme and cover with cold water.
3. Cover saucepan and bring to a boil. Reduce heat and simmer for 25–30 minutes until lentils are tender. Drain mixture, discarding bay leaf and thyme.
4. Toss lentils in butter and season with salt and pepper. Skin sausage and cut into ½-inch slices. Ladle lentils into warm bowls and place a few slices of sausage on top. Serve accompanied by mostarda di Cremona.

Creamed Salt Cod

Baccalà mantecato

Serves 8–10

Salt cod is found in the cooking of many regions of Italy, if not all over the Mediterranean. The fish is salted on the ship after being caught and is then dried on land. This is the version we enjoyed at Enoteca Cul de Sac, spread on toasted bread. In Australia and the United States you can buy salt cod at good Italian and Greek delicatessens.

13 ounces salt cod, in chunks
water
4 medium-sized waxy potatoes (such as fingerling or Finns)
6 unpeeled cloves garlic
⅓ cup cream
1 tablespoon finely chopped Italian parsley
5 tablespoons extra-virgin olive oil
juice of 2 lemons
sea salt
freshly ground black pepper
sourdough bread

1. Soak cod in cold water for 24 hours, changing water 3–4 times.
2. In a saucepan, cover cod with cold water and bring to a boil. Strain boiling water off and replace with more cold water. Repeat this process twice, then simmer for approximately 10 minutes.
3. While cod is cooking, boil potatoes. Roast garlic cloves at 350°F until tender, about 15 minutes. Peel potatoes while still warm and remove skin from garlic. Push potatoes and garlic through a sieve and reserve.
4. When cod is cooked, break apart, removing any bones and skin. Fold into mashed potato and garlic mixture. Mix in cream, parsley, and 3 tablespoons of the olive oil. Add lemon juice to taste and season with salt and pepper. Refrigerate.
5. Just before serving, preheat oven to 350°F. Slice bread and brush with remaining olive oil. Toast in oven, turning to ensure each slice is evenly browned.
6. Serve creamed cod in a decorative bowl, providing knives for spreading it on the bread.

Statue of the She-Wolf

Highlights of the Day

Gail

Kevin

Simon

Robert

The Forum
Walk through these bewitching fields of ruins, take your time and let your imagination do the rest. Temple of Saturn, Temple of Julius Caesar, Column of Phocas. You can almost hear the chariots, taste the ancient wine, and hail Caesar.

Italian Wine Laws
Denominazione di Origine Controllata (DOC) is the official governmental regulation that controls the production of wines in Italy. An extra word, Garantita, indicates a higher level of excellence (DOCG). In recent years, Indicazioni Geografiche Tipiche has been added, creating a distinction between DOC wines and simple table wines.

Hip Rome
In Via del Corso we encountered a street parade. All the young of Rome were packed into the street, hanging out, parading, preening, and being seen. Bring your Vespa, bring your dog, but make sure you wear that new Versace outfit.

Prosciutto di Parma
I always look carefully at prosciutto before buying. Each ham reflects the individuality of its makers, so no two are alike. Older hams often taste of the earth, with a pleasant mustiness and a more assertive saltiness, while younger versions can have a scent of fresh-cut hay.

To Market, to Market

Sunday, May 23

Eight a.m. and coffee in the hotel lounge. Everyone looks a little tired. We decide to take it easy today and rest before we fly south.

A quick taxi ride takes us to Porta Portese, the famous Sunday flea market. This market began at the end of World War II, reportedly growing out of a thriving black market. It is full of tourists and locals, all hunting for a bargain. The rows of stalls go on for miles, towered over by just as many miles of very ordinary-looking apartments. Here there is not the romantic feast of beautiful people and shops as in the old part of Rome. It's actually good to realize that some Romans wear sweatpants to go shopping. They're not all chic.

The Porta Portese trick is to bargain, offer half of what they're asking and pretend to walk away. I hate bargaining and many of the stallholders are obviously sick of tourists and quite aggressive. The others are happy when I suggest we leave after a couple of hours. If you visit this market, beware—wear a money belt and keep your eyes open.

We hop in a cab as no one is thrilled about lots of walking today. It's very hot. We go back to Campo de' Fiori to look at the Sunday antique market. It's friendly, full of old wares, flowers, paintings and handicrafts—an amazing transition from yesterday's abundance of produce, but every bit as charming as the food market. Kevin buys a 1950s fish-shaped bottle opener; Simon a bronze sculpture of Rome's emblem, the She-Wolf; Robert an old soup ladle; and me—I've already purchased in the past two days more than will fit in our suitcase.

We eat panini and little sandwiches with salami and mozzarella. The day is sunny and the sights are sensuous. Tanned Romans of all ages walking, talking, shopping, eating, shouting, laughing—they are so animated and handsome. I'm sure it's rubbing off on Robert; he is becoming more Italian by the day. In fact, it is only being with us that makes him not belong. Otherwise he could just as easily live above the bread shop in front of us.

Using Caterina's local knowledge we head off to find a place for lunch and more film for Simon. Down Via di Pellegrino, onto Via della Coreno Vecchio, slightly west of Piazza Navona, away from the bustle of tourists and into the local thriving lifestyle. How I love the sound of the people's voices.

I've become a dog maniac without Beau around. Look, there's one! We ask if Simon can take a photo. Everyone says yes, with pride that we want to snap their dog. I ask the dogs' names and console myself with pats and chats. Today's names include Lola, Choo Choo, Rex, and Sofia.

No luck finding any of the places Caterina suggested. They are probably behind shutters, closed for Sunday lunch, so back we go to Cul de Sac wine bar where we dined last night. A wine list of 400–500 wines, casual, friendly waiters that are the Italian version of waiters at St. Kilda cafes in Melbourne or Soho waiters in New York (fashionable, tattoos and piercing) and brilliant, simple antipasto and good-tasting food, the best so far. We start feverishly talking and writing down ideas we could use at Donovans. I love the smoked tuna, Kevin the *baccalà* (see page 21), Robert the broad beans and artichokes, and Simon's favorite is the wild-boar pâté. We eat and drink a little more than expected, having a ball together.

It is time for an afternoon nap and preliminary packing for our very early start and the trip down south tomorrow. Realizing we will never be able to fit everything into our one case, Kevin, Robert, and Simon hit the shops in search of additional large carry bags, while I continue to sort through the packing.

Dinner tonight is at a trattoria called La Torricella, at the other end of town, a recommendation of the owner of Enoteca Cul de Sac. It's the equivalent of a neighborhood cafe or diner, a place to eat for locals. What a treat to be able to intrude. Couples, big groups, people dining alone: a cross-section of the neighborhood just doing what all Italians love to do—eating.

Once seated, we wait for instructions on what to do next. Two bottles of wine—one red, one white—and water arrive without choice and there is not a menu in sight, just a simple "What would you like?"

I go for the recommended fish of the day, but Kevin is determined to have the famous Roman pasta dish, rigatoni all'Amatriciana. Simon joins Kevin, and Robert goes for the pasta with artichokes. The self-serve antipasto is a treat while we wait for main courses to be prepared. We taste a wafer-thin tomato-and-cheese-laden pizza that turns out to be a highlight, as is the Caprese salad. Between mouthfuls of food we drink the house wines, a Frascati and a Castelli Romani, both very, very drinkable.

Our main courses are a triumph of home cooking with the best-quality ingredients. Even the owner, roaming the room with her lollipop-pink apron, voluptuous figure, and gold sandals, adds to the atmosphere.

Back to the hotel for our last night's sleep in Rome and a check of plans for the trip tomorrow. South we go!

Gail

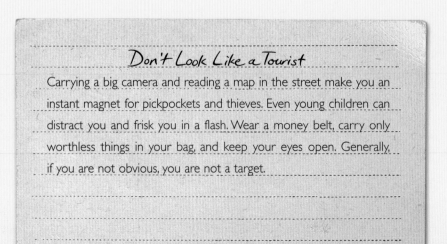

Don't Look Like a Tourist

Carrying a big camera and reading a map in the street make you an instant magnet for pickpockets and thieves. Even young children can distract you and frisk you in a flash. Wear a money belt, carry only worthless things in your bag, and keep your eyes open. Generally, if you are not obvious, you are not a target.

Le avventure di
Pinocchio
di C. Collodi

con illustrazioni
animate di
R. ALBERTARELLI

Edizioni Cavallo

Tomato Salad with Buffalo-milk Mozzarella

Insalata caprese

Serves 4

2 large, very ripe tomatoes
sea salt
pinch of sugar
12 ounces buffalo-milk mozzarella (youngest available)
5–6 tablespoons extra-virgin olive oil
freshly ground black pepper
fresh basil leaves

1. Cut tomatoes into slices approximately ¼ inch thick. Arrange on a flat dish. Sprinkle with sea salt and sugar to extract acids.
2. Allow to stand for 30 minutes, then transfer to a decorative platter.
3. Slice mozzarella the same thickness as tomato and place a slice on top of each tomato slice.
4. Drizzle with olive oil and season with salt and pepper. Garnish each "stack" of tomato and cheese with 1 basil leaf to serve.

Pasta in the Lover's Style

Rigatoni all'Amatriciana

Serves 4

Originating in the town of Amatrice near the Sabine hills, this dish has become a standard of Roman cooking. We fondly call it "in the lover's style" because of the story that the men of Rome were enraptured by the beauty of the women of Amatrice. Rigatoni is much loved in Rome because its ribs and tubular shape trap sauce perfectly.

5 quarts water
4 tablespoons salt
¼ cup olive oil
7 ounces pancetta, diced
1 red bird's-eye chili (or to taste)
1 medium-sized onion, minced
2 cloves garlic, finely chopped
3 medium-sized very ripe tomatoes, peeled, seeded, and
   cut into strips
sea salt
freshly ground black pepper
1 pound good-quality rigatoni
1 cup freshly grated pecorino romano

1. Bring water and salt to a boil.
2. Meanwhile, heat 1 tablespoon of olive oil and fry pancetta slowly over medium heat with chili. When browned, remove pancetta with a slotted spoon and reserve.
3. Add remaining olive oil and sauté onion and garlic with chili until light brown. Add tomato and simmer for 10–15 minutes. Remove chili and discard. Return pancetta to sauce. Season.
4. Cook rigatoni until al dente. Drain well but do not rinse.
5. Toss pasta with sauce and pecorino in a serving bowl. Adjust seasoning and serve with additional cheese if desired.

Cul de Sac wine bar

Highlights of the Day

Gail

Kevin

Simon

Robert

Creative Packing

There was just no way we could carry the large wine bucket we had bought for Donovans. Kevin and Simon tried shops, restaurants, our hotel, the post office—we could not find a packing box. Simon was the hero of the day, seen late in the afternoon sifting through the garbage in the back streets of Via Roma. And so the wine bucket was sent on its way home in a greasy grissini box.

Italian Wine Labels

Navigating an Italian wine label can be a difficult task. Many are named after a location, e.g., Frascati; others carry the grape variety with a place name, e.g., Aglianico del Vulture, which is a red wine made from aglianico grapes, produced in the mountain town of Rionero in Vulture, in Basilicata. Others have a romantic story behind their name, like Est! Est!! Est!!! (see page 33).

When in Rome, Bring Your Dog

Big ones, little ones, young ones, old ones—cani are everywhere in Rome. Where do they live? In the apartments? Hounds, lap-dogs, wolves, bug-eyed monster dogs, pairs of Scottie dogs, gaggles of poodles—anything goes here. When in Rome, bring your dog—or at least buy a chic new collar from Gucci for your dog back at home!

Inexpensive Lunch in Rome

Near Piazza Navona is a fine area for inexpensive little trattorias. Stay away from the main piazza, where the restaurants tend to exploit tourists, and venture into the alleys for eats. True to local Roman standards, Piazza Pasquino and the intersecting streets offer some particularly homey little places.

CONTE ZANDOTTI

Tenimento San Paolo

FRASCATI

Denominazione di origine controllata

SUPERIORE

Via di Colle Mattia, 8
Roma

Tenimento San Paolo
Italia

Imbottigliato dal Viticoltore

CANTINE CONTE ZANDOTTI

750 ml e   PRODOTTO IN ITALIA   12% vol.

Frascati wine achieves a unique ripeness of flavor due to partial fermentation in contact with the skins. The dry version is silky-soft with generous fruit overtones.

Wines of Rome and Lazio

The wines of Lazio (the region in which Rome is situated) have steadily declined in quality over recent years. One theory is that the unavailability of pure drinking water has driven Romans to consume wine as a substitute, almost more per capita than any other place in Italy. Since the market is so competitive and the Romans want their wine at such inexpensive prices, sadly, quality has suffered.

The majority of wine in Lazio is produced in the hills of Castelli Romani, southeast of Rome. The wines are almost all white and dry in style, with Frascati being the most popular. The dry version is silky-soft with generous fruit overtones, and it is also produced in a sweet dessert style called *cannellino*.

We had the opportunity to sample several bottles of Frascati while in Rome. Try to find Frascati Superiore Vigna dei Preti from Villa Simone. The 1998 is a superb example of the style—ample in fruit on the nose with a beautiful freshness on the palate. Conte Zandotti's Frascati Superiore 1998 is more subtly perfumed and an elegant style. Our wine waiter at Enoteca Cul de Sac told us that it would reach its optimum enjoyment level in 3–4 years. With dessert we sampled a glass of the sweeter version, the Frascati Superiore Cannellino 1998 from Villa Simone. This is an extremely interesting wine, sweet and intense with hints of honey. It possesses a subtle oily quality without being cloying.

The other white to try in Lazio is Est! Est!! Est!!! While many connoisseurs scoff at this wine, it can range from remarkably pleasant to downright good. There is an interesting folk tale about the name. It is said that a German bishop sent an advance scout along the route of his impending trip to Rome to search for inns where the wine was good. The scout was to chalk the word—*Est* ("It is") on each location he found. At Montefiascone, the scout liked the wine to much that he inscribed the word in triplicate. Once the bishop arrived, he so loved the wine that he canceled the rest of his trip and stayed in Montefiascone until his death. Try the ones from Falesco: the 1998 offers a lovely freshness. But the best is the Poggio dei Gelsi 1998: rich, fruity, and elegant with a lengthy finish.

Red wines are available, although few and far between. Look for Castelli Romani Rosso from Gotto d'Oro. It is fragrant, soft, and exceptionally easy to drink. Another red is Montiano, from Falesco. The 1996 is a wonderful merlot blend of great intensity and complexity, full of red berries with deep undertones of spice and chocolate. This is a must-have for red-wine lovers.

Kevin

Società An. Italiana

Via Bolli N.

Società An. Italiana
di Assicurazioni e Riassicurazioni

R. ACCA

Registrato
Ricevuta
5234

Sulla presente busta devono ap-
plicarsi francobolli per l'importo
complessivo delle seguenti tasse:
1. Francatura e raccomanda-
zione del piego.
2. Francatura e raccomanda-
zione della ricevuta di ritorno.
La presente raccomandata deve
esser consegnata al do-
micilio od al servi-
zio di recapito
purché trattasi
mente e di età
tredici anni.

Stamperia Reale di Roma 1341

Egregio Signore

Signor Melchiorre Chiappella

(Stroppo)

(Genova per la)

Daria.

31.1.26
NAPOLI-PIENZA-TARANTO

1.2.23
TRANSITO

30 gennaio 1926

NAPOLI-POT...

ESPRESSO
CENT. 60

Cent. 5
QUIRINALE

Società Italiana
Olii

TELEFONO N. 54

Egr. Sig.

Dottore
Umberto Rossi
Stabilimento Del Gaiso
San Giovanni a Teduccio
(Napoli) Portici

Antoni

Via Bartolome

ESPRESSO

MILANO
20-VII-3
1923
PARTENZA

Dottore
Umberto Rossi
Pieno Fortunat
Via due Madre 71
Roma

South to Puglia

Monday, May 24

A 5:30 a.m. start gets us to Fiumicino airport by seven. In typical Italian style, our eight o'clock flight is delayed until 9:30 a.m. While waiting, Robert and I fight our way through the lines of stunning Italian businessmen for coffee. I wonder if all these guys are millionaires or if they just spend every cent they have on clothes, shoes, and eyewear.

Pay first and then take the ticket to the counter is the system. It's Italians at their best—complete chaos, all pushing and yelling, some taking their coffee elsewhere to drink, others drinking at the counter without blinking an eye surrounded by the mad coffee-less mob. It's a theater performance that deserves an encore or two.

We fly south to the city of Brindisi in the region of Puglia (Apulia), near the heel of the boot of Italy. We are all strapped up in our money belts and by the time I load in tickets, passport, cash, traveler's checks, and credit cards mine feels like a bad corset. Even if I breathe in, it bulges.

There's a problem with the rented car at Brindisi, but eventually Robert sorts it out and we squeeze in. Kevin is driving, with Robert giving traffic alerts beside him, and Simon and I, the navigators, are in the back. Kevin's been so excited about getting behind the wheel—it's my worst

nightmare, but I hang in there and try to look in control, like everyone else.

From the moment we head down the road, Kevin becomes "Fangio," after the famous racing-car driver. He's so happy. We are all laughing. Before we know it we have reached our first destination—Lecce. Simon visited here some five years ago, and it's his dream town. We have booked a day rate at Patria Palace hotel, where we leave the car, load our bags into the single room, freshen up, and put our precious goodies in a safety deposit box. We are now free to wander without leaving the car vulnerable to robbery. Normally we would stay for the night, but time doesn't allow.

The staff at the hotel suggest a place for lunch where we can have authentic food. They book us a table at Ristorante Alle Due Corti and off we go to explore the wonders of Lecce. It is even more beautiful than Simon has told us. Just 7 miles from the Adriatic Sea and 15 miles from the Ionian Sea, it is the primary town of the Salentine Peninsula and has been described as the Florence of the south. Lecce has Greek heritage and later became an important part of the Roman Empire. It also has a history as a center of scholarship and much of the architecture in the old town is seventeenth-century Baroque. One magnificent piazza after another—breathtaking. We have blue skies, warm weather, and Simon as our tour guide. When you visit a town you remember and love, you almost take ownership of it, and so it is with Simon. Every building looks like an overdone Italian wedding cake, but the town is full of very stylish people. It is still a student town, with excellent shopping and very groovy bars.

We stop by the bishop's palace—what a blissful life the monks must lead. Their private piazza has its very own Baroque wishing well, and it must be lovely to sit and take in the beauty and tranquillity of the surroundings before morning prayers in the adjoining cathedral.

At lunch we are overwhelmed by the hospitality we receive from Roselba and Daniello De Carlo. The authentic cooking coupled with the charm of the restaurant and its owners make it a meal to remember. Kevin experiences for the first time real Italian home-style cooking and, more importantly, the passion of the local people. They say the way to a man's heart is through his stomach, and this is living proof. Kevin is so taken by the signora and the vast quantities of delicious goodies she keeps bringing from the kitchen, it seems at one point he is going to divorce me on the spot and eat forever at Roselba's. Kevin has two nicknames now—Fangio in the car and "Gold-fish" at the table. Let's hope he keeps fitting behind the steering wheel. He's a natural at driving and we all feel confident. No one else wants to take up the challenge of driving in Italy.

We make a bit of a mistake after lunch, leaving the restaurant only to find that Lecce has become a virtual desert. Nothing is open until 4:30 in the afternoon. We had forgotten this tradition, as much of Rome operates throughout the day. Luckily the place we had read about which serves the best granita di caffè, Caffè Alvino on Piazza Sant'Oronzo, is still open. Why not eat more? Robert is still at the restaurant with the signora talking food and recipes, so the three tourists go alone. Caffè Alvino is the coolest place we've been in. Who knows where all these street people come from at 3:00 p.m. on a hot Monday afternoon? They are much less conservative than the Romans, hip hip hip, lots of designer clothes.

The granita di caffè—espresso coffee frozen and stirred until it is an icy mush, served with dollops of fresh whipped cream—is a delight. I thought I asked for it without cream, a diet-conscious decision just after the lunch we've had, but it comes with a mountain of the stuff. Oh well, in my desire to be super-cool in such a hip cafe I probably made a mistake when I ordered.

There is no time to wait for the shops to open. We need to find our evening stop, Galatone. If you ever go to Lecce we can recommend you make time to stay long enough to enjoy the town and explore the shopping. All

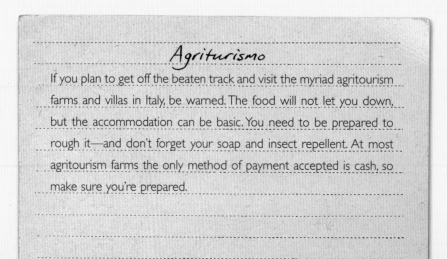

Agriturismo

If you plan to get off the beaten track and visit the myriad agritourism farms and villas in Italy, be warned. The food will not let you down, but the accommodation can be basic. You need to be prepared to rough it—and don't forget your soap and insect repellent. At most agritourism farms the only method of payment accepted is cash, so make sure you're prepared.

At Alle Due Corti, Roselba serves and explains her wonderful food

Lecce street

Baroque balcony

Lecce town emblem

the designer stores are here, along with the very best in food and wine shopping. Everything about Lecce is special, even the town emblem of a dog surrounded by acorns—we loved it all.

Fangio is back behind the wheel and we're off to Galatone, about 19 miles from Lecce. We have booked to stay at an *agriturismo* (agritourism) farm—a working farm with rooms available for rent—and the first of many such places we plan to visit. Masseria Lo Prieno is well known for homegrown produce and excellent food prepared by a mother-and-daughter team. The trip is fine and we are there in 40 minutes, unpacked, and out and about. Simon, with his camera, is surrounded by prickly pear, ancient olive groves, dry-stone walls, dust, and very hot sun. Robert is wandering through the grapevines and cherry trees.

Time for dinner. Mama Castriota cooks out the back in the kitchen while Maria Grazia serves and explains all the dishes. It is completely wonderful, everything made with love and tradition—fresh pecorino, yogurt, and potato mash, homemade semidried olives, and limoncello. The highlight is the hand-rolled tortelli with ricotta and nettles. You could make the trip for this alone.

We are all in bed by 9:30 p.m. The surroundings are beautiful but the apartment is minimal. The four of us are tired, cramped, falling all over our luggage. Nonetheless, any discomfort can be completely overlooked when you taste such food.

Gail

The well at the Bishop's Seminary in Lecce

Warm Potatoes with Chili and Pecorino Romano

Patate della nonna

Serves 4

This wonderfully simple dish was served at Ristorante Alle Due Corti.

1 bird's-eye chili
¼–⅓ cup extra-virgin olive oil
4–5 medium-sized waxy potatoes (fingerling, if possible)
salt
sea salt
freshly ground black pepper
pecorino romano
freshly chopped Italian parsley

1. Slice the chili and stir into olive oil, with seeds. Set aside.
2. Cover the potatoes with generously salted cold water and bring to a boil. Reduce heat and simmer until tender.
3. Drain potatoes and allow to cool slightly. Peel while still warm and cut into ¼-inch slices.
4. Arrange potato slices on a serving plate. Drizzle with chili-flavored olive oil and season with sea salt and pepper. Sprinkle with parsley. With a vegetable peeler, shave pecorino romano in slices over the top and serve immediately.

Bucatini with Cherry Tomatoes, Garlic, and Chili

Pasta con pomodorini

Serves 4

Roselba said that this was one of her favorite Pugliese pasta preparations. As the cherry tomatoes become superheated, they scatter around the pan until their skins burst. Bucatini is a long, thin pasta similar to spaghetti but with a hollow center.

5 quarts water
salt
1 pound good-quality bucatini pasta
2 cloves garlic, finely chopped
⅓ cup extra-virgin olive oil
2 bird's-eye chilies, sliced
1 pound very ripe red and yellow cherry tomatoes
12 basil leaves, coarsely chopped
sea salt
freshly ground black pepper
1 cup freshly grated pecorino romano

1. Bring water and 4 tablespoons salt to a boil. Cook bucatini until al dente.
2. Meanwhile, using the back of a knife, mash garlic with 1 teaspoon salt until a paste is formed.
3. In a skillet or frying pan, warm olive oil and add garlic paste and chili and begin to soften but do not brown. Add cherry tomatoes and roll in pan over high heat until skins pop, about 2–3 minutes.
4. Drain pasta well but do not rinse. Reserve 1–2 tablespoons of pasta water to add to sauce.
5. Add drained bucatini to sauce with reserved pasta water. Add basil, sea salt, and pepper and simmer for a few minutes.
6. Serve all at once in a large bowl, accompanied by grated pecorino romano.

Masseria Lo Prieno and its ancient olive groves

Highlights of the Day

Gail

Kevin

Simon

Robert

Fangio

I couldn't believe how happy and at ease Kevin was behind the wheel. We had a Renault station wagon carrying four passengers and 400 tons of luggage (slight exaggeration). I knew Kevin would have fun in Italy, I just didn't know how much. I was worried he'd never want to go home! That's mio caro.

Lunch at Ristorante Alle Due Corti

Words cannot describe how enchanting this experience was! Roselba De Carlo grabbed my hand and dragged me to the kitchen to show me what she had prepared for the day's fare. The highlight was the bucatini pasta tossed with cherry tomatoes cooked in oil just until their skins popped. It is in this setting, this culture, that one can appreciate the beauty of the seasons and food as a joy of life, not just a means to an end.

A Wonderful Town

Lecce was the very first town I went to on my first trip to Italy, and it will always be one of my favorites. It is seriously beautiful with its breathtaking Baroque stonework. Wander around the old part of town, but keep your wits about you—you might need to jump into a doorway to avoid being taken around town on the front of a Vespa.

Fico d'India

The prickly pear is so popular in southern Italy. The Italian name comes from its botanical name, Opuntia ficus-india, meaning the American Indian fig—it originated in Central America. A variety of cactus which grows wild everywhere, it has a very strong taste. The yellow ones taste of banana, while the red ones taste of pear with a hint of strawberry. A southern Italian breakfast isn't complete without them.

43

Bottom of the Boot

Tuesday, May 25

We start the day beautifully, with the most delicious "fat-free" breakfast you can imagine. To me this is the highlight of our stay at Lo Prieno. Freshly baked crunchy and soft rolls, eaten with homemade mandarin preserves with the most delicious peel I have ever tasted—certainly not anything like my grandma ever made—and jam made with cherries dried in the sun for 40 days. What a flavor. Then there are sweet pastries filled with custard cream *(bocconetti)* which are a typical confection of Puglia, chocolate-coated celebration cakes, and a pot of steaming caffè latte. I worked so hard to lose 10 pounds before I left Australia, and I've just eaten enough to put it all back on. But it's worth every mouthful.

We leave our luggage at the farm while we travel to Otranto for lunch. This seaside fishing town is way down in the heel of Italy and famous for its churches and mosaics. The trip is simple and the Adriatic Coast is at its finest. We see the vibrant water for the first time; blue, aqua, cobalt, and green shining in the sun.

In Otranto we head for the *centro storico*, the historic part. A towering wall surrounds the old town. Simon is our guide again as he's visited Otranto before. Robert is off down to the fishing co-op to check out the seafood. Kevin stumbles on a wine shop extraordinaire, Enoteca Massafra Daniele, which has every wine he has been reading about. We later discover he has bought six bottles for us to taste—I'm sure we can arrange that.

Simon and I stroll along the main street in search of things to throw our *lire* at. Now we are in pottery country, and oh, how I love this stuff. The shops spill onto the street with bowls, plates, platters, and dinner sets. Despite my longings, Simon keeps me sensible and we only purchase a salad bowl.

We catch up with the others and climb the steep roads to Otranto's famous cathedral. It's breathtaking, although the crypt is a bit creepy for my liking.

Back in the village we find that the gelato shop Kevin has on his list is closed, but the young man sitting in the sun opposite offers to open up for us. They are very friendly here. We choose chocolate, tiramisu, panna cotta, pistachio, and coffee. Nothing is overly sweet, and the vital flavor of the ingredients is left to shine through.

What pigs we are, eating gelato while we look for somewhere to have lunch. After a stroll around we choose Ristorante Da Sergio, which belongs to the owner of the ice-cream shop. Everything else that looks worthwhile is closed. I can't figure it out. In Lecce most of the restaurants were closed on Monday; here it is a Tuesday closing.

The owner explains that many businesses are still closed for winter and won't open until 1 June, a week from now, when the holiday season starts.

We have moved from one side of the heel of the boot to the other, and the food has taken on the main influence of the area—seafood. As we expected, fish is dominating our dining in the south. We have chosen a great restaurant here. The antipasto and selection of grilled fish are in a class of their own. So fresh, so sweet. There is a touch of chili finding its way into the food and a few things are dusted, such as mussels and calamari. The wine is having a great effect, and we are all laughing about nothing. The tables, on a dark timber terrace, are covered in linen mixed and matched in pale lemon, coffee, and crisp white colors. Stunning. Overhead, a canopy of woven sticks shades us from the sun. What a place, what a lunch.

Back to Galatone to collect our luggage and head for another agritourism farm, in Monopoli, 25 miles from Brindisi on the other side of the heel. We have chosen these destinations for their culture, regional produce, and cuisine. They also enable us to skirt around the volatile, busy cities and experience real regional foods.

The coast road into Monopoli is superb, with small towns and seaside resorts, restaurants and beachside lidos. We arrive at Masseria Curatori, the home of Onofrio Contento, his wife, and their three sons. The house is a huge, double-story villa washed in rose-pink, surrounded by ancient olive trees, beautiful cows, and lots of dogs. It is completely captivating, as is the family who owns it.

Our rooms are through a wrought-iron gate which opens onto an old walled garden full of roses, lemons, and grapevines, leading to a large, comfortable apartment. It is more peaceful and magical than I ever imagined from the magazine article that led us here. We rest and shelter from the heat under the vines, sampling some of Kevin's wine purchases, and then make our way to the main house for dinner.

The whole family joins us around the table with only Robert translating, plus my broken Italian and Fangio's *ciao tutti*. We eat, drink, and somehow all talk to each other nonstop until the early hours of the morning. The dinner is a perfect example of home cooking using the produce of Puglia. With such wonderful vegetable dishes, you don't even notice that there is no meat. What a heavenly place for vegetarians. The highlights are homemade pecorino, the best tomatoes we've ever tasted, Robert's face while he talks to Signora Contento about her food, Kevin sampling the homemade wines and liqueurs, the bread, and the handmade pasta with just enough tomato to coat, not drown. We stagger to bed, tired and full and content like our hosts, delighted we have another night here.

Through the open bedroom window I can smell newly turned earth and hear a chorus of weird animal noises and someone snoring. I lie awake, worried that some strange beast will jump through the window any second. Then the limoncello liqueur wins, and I drift off to sleep.

Gail

Mosquitoes

It's great being in the middle of nowhere, without a shop in sight. However, when the weather is hot, open windows are a must. If you plan to do the agritourism thing, take every kind of mosquito ammunition you can find. They're bad!

A window in the old town of Otranto

Our first sight of the blue water of the Adriatic

47

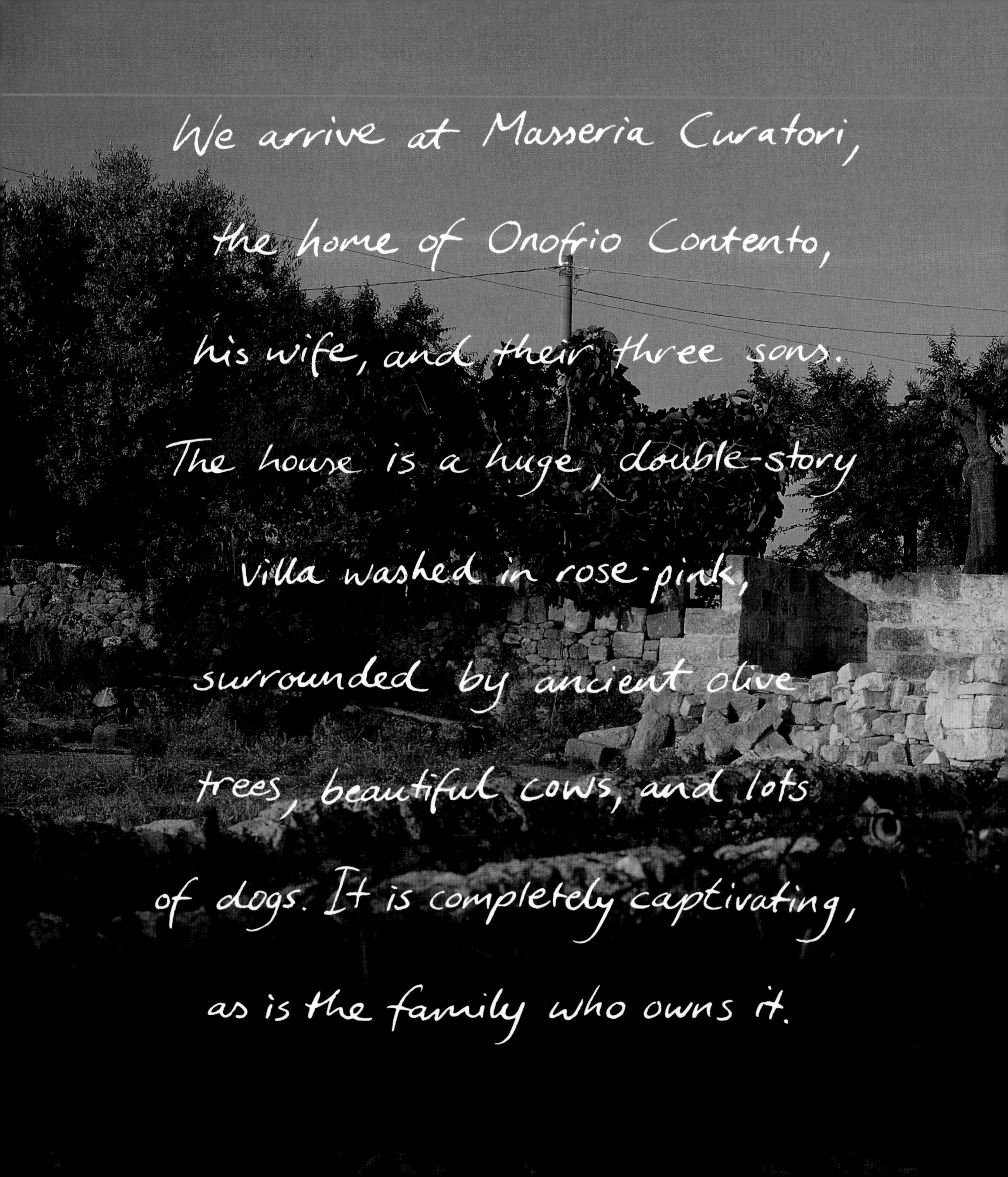

We arrive at Masseria Curatori,

the home of Onofrio Contento,

his wife, and their three sons.

The house is a huge, double-story

villa washed in rose-pink,

surrounded by ancient olive

trees, beautiful cows, and lots

of dogs. It is completely captivating,

as is the family who owns it.

Resting under the vines at Masseria Curatori

Mandarin Marmalade

Marmalata al mandarino

Makes approximately 4 cups

With Maria Grazia's mandarin marmalade made from the fruit of the farm, breakfast at Masseria Lo Prieno was a treat.

12 medium-sized mandarins
1½ cups water
sugar
⅓ cup lemon juice
¼ cup Cointreau

1. Cut mandarins into thirds. Place them in a bowl and cover with water. Let stand overnight.
2. Next day, transfer mandarins and water to a saucepan and bring to a boil. Reduce heat and simmer, covered, until rind is soft, approximately 30 minutes.
3. Measure fruit and water as a number of cups. Return mixture to saucepan and add 1 cup of sugar for each measured cup of fruit and water. Stir over heat, without boiling, until sugar dissolves.
4. Stir in lemon juice and bring to a boil. Boil uncovered, without stirring, for approximately 30 minutes until mixture gels when tested. (To test, put a teaspoon of hot mixture on a chilled saucer and place in refrigerator for a few minutes. Run your finger through mixture as if your finger is a knife and you are cutting mixture in half. If mixture remains as 2 separate pieces, marmalade is ready.)
5. Stir in Cointreau and let stand for 10 minutes. Store marmalade in lidded jars that have been sterilized in boiling water for 10 minutes and dried in the oven at 350°F. Pour marmalade into hot jars and seal when completely cool.

Grilled Fish with Green Sauce

Pesce alla griglia con salsa verde

Serves 4

Grilling is a cooking technique that has existed for thousands of years and is a favored method in nearly every culinary culture. Add a twist by experimenting with fresh herbs scattered over the coals just before grilling to impart interesting flavors to the finished product.

4 x 7-ounce fillets of firm, oily fish (swordfish, marlin, *or* salmon)
olive oil
sea salt
freshly ground black pepper
sprigs of fresh herbs such as rosemary, basil, sage, *or* juniper
    (optional)

SALSA VERDE
1 slice casalinga bread
½ cup red-wine vinegar
1 cup Italian parsley leaves
2 cloves garlic
4 anchovies
1 tablespoon capers
yolk of 1 hard-boiled egg
1 cup extra-virgin olive oil
sea salt
freshly ground black pepper

1. To make salsa verde, soak bread in red-wine vinegar for 20–30 minutes. In a mortar and pestle, combine parsley, garlic, anchovies, and capers until a smooth paste is achieved. Add egg yolk and mix with a wooden spoon until smooth. Squeeze soaked bread dry and add to mortar and pestle.
2. Add oil slowly, mixing with a small whisk or fork. The sauce will develop a lovely creamy texture. Adjust seasoning and refrigerate, covered, for 1 hour before serving. This quantity makes 1½–2 cups. Salsa verde can be kept, refrigerated, for up to 1 week.
3. Preheat barbecue or overhead grill for 15–20 minutes. Brush fish liberally with olive oil and season with salt and pepper.
4. If using a barbecue, sprinkle herbs directly onto hot coals or surface of grill. When herbs begin to smoke, set fish on grill and cook for about 3 minutes on each side.
5. Serve immediately, accompanied by salsa verde.

Highlights of the Day

Gail

Kevin

Simon

Robert

The Big Pink House

Something magical happened to me here. I suppose it was because I realized, after almost a week, that I was on vacation. The day-to-day pressure of running a busy restaurant with a big staff was too far away to worry about. I was under the spell of the big pink house.

The Wines of Southern Italy

When thinking of Italian wines, the more famous selections from the north spring to mind, such as Barolo, Chianti, and the super-Tuscans. But the much-maligned wines of the south are having a resurgence. Modern techniques have led the comeback and southern Italy is becoming known for very good wines with exceptional value.

Churches in Otranto

The Byzantine murals in the chapel in Otranto are a little rustic but well worth a look. The cathedral has a mosaic floor with scenes from mythology and the Bible, and don't miss the side chapel, which shows all too graphically some of the savage history of the town, with the remains of hundreds of people neatly stacked in glass cases.

The Seafood Co-op

In the late afternoon, when the sun was not so strong, there was a continuous line of different-sized fishing boats returning home after a long day at sea. The lucky ones with full wooden boxes went inside the market and began bidding. The fishermen were all trying to get the best prices for their catch, and this created a very chaotic and passionate scene all'Italiana!

CHEESE SHOP-LOCOROTONDO - BURRATA

The Taste of Contentment

Wednesday, May 26

Everyone congregates in the main house for breakfast. There is everything Puglia can offer—cherry jam, quince jam, exquisite pastries, home-fired bread, and caffè latte served in a huge pot. The highlight is a freshly baked sponge-like cake, not sweet and with a rich yellow color from the farm eggs. I can't believe I ate three pieces—I hope we never have time to go swimming when we travel further south! The idea of trying to look decent in a swimsuit is horrific. Obviously not horrific enough to stop me from eating, for we are soon off to the nearby towns for lunch, hoping to be back early enough for a tour of the Contento farm.

We head for Martina Franca and Alberobello, towns famous for their enchanting *trulli* architecture, pasta, and bread-making. A couple of wrong turns and we find our way. At Kevin's insistence we stop to buy *burrata*, a cheese he wants to sample. Two gooey white balls are purchased to eat with dinner tonight.

But how will we keep the cheese cold? Unfortunately we can't leave it at the shop to pick up again on our way back to the farm, because as usual the shops close at 12:30 p.m. and don't reopen until 4:30 p.m., by which time we'll be long gone. And of course we didn't think to bring a cooler along. I get an idea and we stop again in a small

town to purchase a towel, which I dip into the town-square fountain and then use to wrap the cheese in. It then goes into a plastic shopping bag, just like my mother wrapped food up when we were kids. When you are prepared to make a complete fool of yourself by looking as though you are taking a bath in the local fountain, that's love. As an obvious tourist, I drew a crowd!

We drive onward up into the hills to Martina Franca to visit the village's famous food shops. At the fascinating butcher's shop, tripe is the day's special. The pasta shop is full of orecchiette, the little ear-shaped pasta typical of Puglia. The bread here is dense and delicious, and the crowded bread shop is a testament to its quality.

We stumble on a market and seize the chance to stock up on necessities. Soap and laundry detergent are essential as there has been no clothes washing for five days—Rome didn't have laundry service on the weekend, and we haven't sighted a Whirlpool in any of the places we've stayed—as are aspirin for the hangovers we all have this morning, tissues for the colds Kevin and I have caught, and insect repellent. We find super sunglasses and beautiful Missoni towels for Kevin's birthday in two days.

Bad planning! We are completely overloaded, as usual, and the car is parked much too far away. We arrive at our lunch destination and the owner kindly offers us a table for eight so as to accommodate our shopping bags.

Trattoria La Cantina, famous for its local cuisine, is down a flight of old stairs and then down again to a beautiful, domed, stone-lined room. The four little pigs are starting to be a little more careful about what we order. Until today we have ordered the antipasto and been prepared to take what we get. It is usually perfect, but there is often too much of it. We try to be more selective here, but fail because we make the mistake of telling the owner we have a restaurant in Australia. The roasted peppers, tripe, calamari, and fried mushrooms we did not order arrive anyway. Oh well, it's all delicious and goes down easily with jugs of Martina Franca's rosso and bianco wines. Highlights of the meal are fried baby cod, almost like whitebait, and orecchiette with fresh peas. We are bursting, but the owner brings quince-filled pastries. A must, he says.

The day is slipping away and Simon convinces us to give Alberobello a miss. He's been there before and says it's very touristy. Of course, we don't consider ourselves tourists! Instead we take a shortcut home through Locorotondo, where there are plenty of pretty *trulli* houses to see, without the souvenir shops. The valley of Locorotondo is truly an incredible sight.

Fabrizio, the youngest son of the Contentos, is back at the farm to meet us. We visit his father milking the cows, surrounded by the three little dogs that roam everywhere, Katie, Jimmy, and Mimi—sort of house dogs that aren't allowed in the house. Then there's the compound with the *vitello* or veal—the calves. It's a little too close to reality for me, and I ask what we are eating tonight. Thankfully not veal! Of course I realize this is the life on a farm, but I'm not used to seeing it. There are also chickens, donkeys, fresh herbs, and vegetables growing everywhere and two huge white dogs called Toby and Zelda, the farm's working dogs. And a yard full of horses for guests to ride.

The beautiful old grotto where they once pressed olive oil is home to a special animal. We wander down past a couple of old walls and there it is: the biggest, whitest Arabian stallion I have ever seen, in his stall for the night. I have always been scared of horses and go weak at the knees with fear. His pink eyes are staring at me. Everyone else thinks he is beautiful, but I head for ground level to escape, hoping no one will notice how frightened I am.

The tour of the main house finds Signora Contento busy preparing what she says will be a very special meal for us. From an earlier discussion about the fine food we had at Masseria Lo Prieno, I presume she has an idea of showing us what her own specialities are. I happened to see her lighting the wood-fired oven early this morning.

Dinner turns out to be the most outstanding meal to date. There is no way to imagine how much work Signora Contento has put into it. We begin with fava beans which have been standing in a terra-cotta pot next to the open

Allow for Getting Lost

Never underestimate how long it takes to find your way around the countryside of Italy. Signage is minimal. Expect to get lost and always allow enough time to reach your evening destination. The pressure of trying to achieve too much in a day will end in certain frustration. Enjoy the view, even if you have no idea where you are. And remember, all roads lead to Rome.

flame of the outdoor oven for some seven hours, mashed, and served with braised chicory. It is a taste none of us has experienced before. Antipasto follows, highlighting the farm produce: baby focaccia with onions, beets cooked with mint, dried zucchini, fried pastries filled with tomato, and involtini of eggplant with fresh ricotta and prosciutto, a star of a dish. And it continues: pastries stuffed with fresh mozzarella and olives, pizza with asparagus, frittata with fresh artichokes. We are all astounded at the wonderful food that has been prepared in order to please us.

The main course of beef involtini and roasted pork is served with a simple green salad dressed with the olive oil and vinegar produced on the farm. How can I describe the wonderful taste? The vinegar alone is like wine and limes mixed together. Fresh fruit and the signora's fresh ricotta, made that morning with sea water, provide a triumphant end to a dinner none of us will forget.

When coffee is served we receive another surprise when we discover that the beef involtini was in fact made with horse, a meat quite commonly eaten in this part of Italy. I suddenly realize that even though I dislike horses a lot, I don't hate them enough to eat one. But it's too late now.

We ask Signora Contento about her plans for the future. Who will take over the kitchen when she retires? She smiles and tells us that the kitchen at Masseria Curatori will be *chiuso* (closed)—her three sons don't cook and none of them is married. She explains that even if they *were* married, their wives, like most young Italian women of today, would likely to be much more interested in a career than in cooking. She believes skills such as hers will disappear. We hope not, for they are too precious.

We roll off to bed as full as we can possibly be. I wish I could speak more Italian so I could tell Signora Contento how much we appreciate her cooking, her undying commitment, and how much work she put into the dinner. It's been another dreamy night with the family Contento, and we are content beyond expectations.

Gail

Trattoria La Cantina

On the farm with Fabrizio, son of the Contentos

Signor Contento milks the cows and Signora Contento prepares our evening meal

Eggplant Rolls with Prosciutto and Ricotta

Involtini di melanzane

Makes 12

2 medium-sized eggplants
salt
olive oil
sea salt
freshly ground black pepper
12 slices prosciutto
12 basil leaves
9 ounces ricotta

1. Cut eggplants into ¼-inch slices. Choose 12 slices of equal size and discard the remainder. Salt both sides of slices and let stand for 30 minutes to extract any bitterness. Rinse and pat dry with paper towels. Heat a little olive oil in a skillet or frying pan and fry eggplant over medium heat until golden brown. Drain on a paper towels.

2. Lay eggplant slices on work surface and season with sea salt and pepper. Place 1 slice of prosciutto and 1 basil leaf torn into small pieces on each piece of eggplant.

3. For each eggplant slice, take 1 tablespoon of ricotta and form into a sausage shape. Lay ricotta at one end of eggplant slice and roll involtini up, finishing with seam down. Serve at room temperature, with Tomato Sauce (see page 82), if desired.

60

Little Ear Pasta with Fresh Peas

Orecchiette e piselli

Serves 4

Orecchiette is the traditional pasta of Puglia. The dough consists of durum wheat semolina mixed with water and is hard in texture. Each little ear is formed by hand, pressing down a small amount of dough with the thumb. It is said that one can recognize homemade orecchiette because the impression of the maker's thumbnail can be seen on the inside of the pasta.

3 medium-sized onions, halved and sliced
3–4 tablespoons olive oil
2 cups shelled peas
4 cups chicken stock
salt
5 quarts water
1 pound good-quality orecchiette
4 egg yolks
freshly ground black pepper
freshly grated pecorino romano

1. In a saucepan, fry onion in olive oil gently until translucent. Add peas and toss. Cover with chicken stock, then add a little salt and bring to a boil. Reduce to a rolling simmer and continue cooking until peas are tender, 15 minutes. Drain, reserving cooking liquid.
2. While peas are cooking, pour water into a large pot and add 4 tablespoons salt. Bring to a boil. Cook orecchiette until al dente (it will take slightly longer to cook than other types of pasta because of the denseness of the flour).
3. Drain pasta and combine with peas and enough reserved cooking liquid to form a sauce. Add egg yolks and stir continuously for a few minutes over very high heat to thicken sauce slightly. Do not boil or sauce will turn into scrambled eggs.
4. Adjust seasoning and serve immediately, passing grated cheese.

Roasted Peppers Under Oil

Peperoni sott'olio

Serves 4–6

2 red peppers
2 yellow peppers
2 green peppers
½ cup extra-virgin olive oil
1 tablespoon red-wine vinegar
charred rosemary sticks (optional)
roasted garlic cloves (optional)
sea salt
freshly ground black pepper

1. Preheat oven broiler to hot. Cut peppers, into quarters and remove stalk end, internal ribs, and seeds. Place skin-side up on a tray and broil until skins begin to blister and blacken. (Do not oil peppers—the oil will burn and impart "off" flavors.)
2. Place peppers in a bowl and cover with plastic wrap for about 15 minutes. Peel, removing all bits of blackened skin.
3. Place in a shallow dish with oil and vinegar. Add rosemary and garlic, if using, and season, turning so that all ingredients are combined.
5. Serve at room temperature. Peppers will keep in the refrigerator, covered, for up to 1 week.

Fava Bean Purée with Sautéed Chicory

Favetta

Serves 4

This dish uses the variety of chicory known as curly endive elsewhere and is one of the most traditional Pugliese dishes. Signora Contento cooked it very slowly in a crock pot on the open fire outside her kitchen. During our farm tour we had all wondered what was in store for us when we saw it bubbling away. This is our version of her treat.

1 pound dried fava beans (about 3½ cups)
⅓ cup olive oil
1 medium-sized onion, diced
salt
freshly ground black pepper
2 pounds chicory (curly endive), stems removed
3 cloves garlic, minced

1. Soak beans in cold water overnight. Remove any that have discolored or floated to the top of soaking liquid, then drain. Place in a pot and pour in cold water to a level of 2 inches above the beans.
2. Heat half the olive oil in a skillet or frying pan and fry onion over low heat until soft.
3. Bring beans to a boil and reduce heat to low. Stir in onion and its oil, cover and cook for 1 hour. Add ½ teaspoon salt and a little pepper. Cook for a further ½–1 hour until beans are tender.
4. While beans are finishing cooking, wash chicory thoroughly and roughly chop leaves. Bring a liberal quantity of salted water to a boil and blanch chicory until just wilted. Refresh under cold water and drain.
5. Drain beans, reserving cooking liquid and a few whole beans. Pass remaining beans through a food mill to remove skins. Season. Add enough reserved cooking liquid to thin purée to a thick, soup-like consistency. Set aside and keep warm.
6. Heat remaining olive oil in a skillet or frying pan and fry garlic over low heat until soft. Increase heat to medium and add chicory, stirring continuously until hot. Season.
7. Divide bean purée among 4 soup plates. Top with sautéed chicory and reserved whole beans. Serve with a cruet of extra-virgin olive oil and some crusty bread.

Signora Contento's Breakfast Cake

Torta di arancia e limone

On our first morning at Masseria Curatori, Signora Contento served this magnificent golden cake full of the scent of oranges and lemons.

2½ cups all-purpose flour
1½ teaspoons baking powder
½ teaspoon baking soda
pinch of salt
zest and juice of 1 orange
zest and juice of 1 lemon
¾ cup milk
1 cup + 2 tablespoons unsalted butter
1¼ cups sugar
1 teaspoon vanilla extract
5 eggs

1. Preheat oven to 350°F. Line a 10-inch cake pan with baking parchment on the bottom and sides.
2. Combine flour, baking powder, baking soda, and salt and sift into a bowl. Add orange and lemon zest. Set aside.
3. Combine orange and lemon juice with milk and set aside.
4. Using an electric mixer with a whisk attachment, cream butter, sugar, and vanilla extract on high speed until light and fluffy. Reduce mixer speed to medium and add eggs 1 at a time, incorporating after each addition. (Because of the quantity of eggs, the mixture will not be completely emulsified—do not be alarmed at this.)
5. Add flour and milk mixtures alternately one-third at a time, incorporating after each addition. Be sure to scrape sides of bowl with a rubber spatula before each addition and after the final addition.
6. Pour batter into lined cake pan and bake until top is golden brown, approximately 50 minutes. Check to see if cake is ready by inserting a toothpick into the center. If it comes out clean, the cake is cooked.
7. Cool on a rack and turn out onto a decorative platter to serve.

Highlights of the Day

Gail

Kevin

Simon

Robert

Down on the Farm

I loved being on the farm for a couple of days. It made me miss our beautiful dog at home. The animals were truly lovely, as was the continuous chorus of barking, mooing, and crowing, and, as if cued by a conductor, the male peacock displaying from the top of the walled garden at sunset.

In Search of Cheese

There is an extremely interesting version of mozzarella found only in Locorotondo. This delicious cheese, called burrata, has a firm skin that opens to a soft, creamy heart. The best way to eat this delicacy is to tear off a piece of the skin and dip it into the liquid center.

Trulli

Can you imagine living in an upturned ice-cream cone constructed of stones? That's probably the closest thing I can think of to a trulli house. Each cone forms a room in the house, with some houses having up to six or eight cones. Everyone you meet seems to have a different story as to the origins of the trulli but no one really knows how they came to be.

Local Produce

In Australia and America people often talk about local produce. In Puglia they don't talk about it, they live it. Every meal we had featured delicious, ingenious dishes, centuries old, and created by the necessity of utilizing everything this dry, hot region has to offer.

Happy Birthday, Fangio

Thursday, May 27

Today is Kevin's birthday and probably the hardest drive of the trip. We make a very early start and a sad breakfast as we say goodbye to the Contento family. Their farm was so good and so inexpensive that it doesn't seem fair that we have paid so little for so much.

We are heading south out of Monopoli to the region of Basilicata and down to our destination, the seaside resort of Maratea. The day's trip will take us from one coast of Italy to the other, from the Adriatic to the Tyrrhenian Sea. Everyone is squashed into the station wagon, chatting, and listening to the radio. Kevin is happy to drive and loves the idea of reaching our first big autostrada.

Progress is good until we turn off the major road onto a smaller one which leads through the mountains and south to the coast. The drive becomes a nightmare. The road is under construction, full of trucks and Vespas and impatient Italian drivers. And what hills! Our ears pop as we climb mountains, in and out of tunnels, over and around tall bridges. We turn off the radio and everyone is silent, eyes riveted to the road. The drivers behind are tooting, so close to our bumper that Simon and I, in the back, feel as though they are sitting with us.

It's a harrowing four-hour drive. The Italians dart in and out of the convoys of trucks that develop, always on the wrong side of the road, and always passing on blind corners. The road goes from one lane to two and back to one and warning signs are rare. We take a pit stop after two hours to have a panini and a coffee and stock up with water, chocolate, snacks, and cassette tapes to pass the time—the radio has disappeared behind the mountains.

Back on the road the saga continues. Fangio is doing a great job, but we know he's under pressure. Our car has a small engine, four people who haven't stopped eating or shopping for a week, and a clutch that has a mind of its own. We couldn't pass a donkey!

Signs for Reggio di Calabria, way down south, appear. The road widens and traffic becomes minimal. At last we can relax a little and look at the scenery. The mountains are all around us as we drive through the valley. Little clusters of whitewashed terra-cotta roofed houses cling to the tops and sides of the mountains. We pass by the village of Rivello. It's tantalizingly picturesque, but regrettably we can't stop everywhere. As we head further into Basilicata it seems our research about the area has left us misinformed. We expected it to be dry, barren, and without character, but the reverse is actually the case. Once over the mountains and down to the Tyrrhenian coast it is lush, green, and full of vines, bougainvillea, and pine trees.

The instructions to Villa Cheta Elite, our destination for tonight, are very vague. They say "Acquafredda di Maratea, 1 km south." South of where? The town of Maratea is spread out down the side of a steep mountain reaching to the sea. We make several attempts to find the road to Acquafredda and wind up back at the same road junction.

By some miracle we come around yet another winding piece of road and recognize the building from an ink sketch in our guidebook. The description of the villa reads: "A liberty-style villa with sienna and cream washed walls." To me it looks more like an apricot-colored doll's house perched on the edge of the cliff. I now understand why our confirmation fax was covered in cherubs. It's certainly busy, and full of amazing bits and pieces. Thank goodness there is a porter here to help us with our bags—there are so many steps up to the rooms. The double French doors and individual balconies for each room are a bonus. It's very romantic, a bit like the film *A Room with a View*, with fine linen curtains blowing in the breeze.

Our host, Lamberto Aquadro, comes to greet us. We wander around the villa, through the sitting rooms and dining rooms, and even into the kitchen to see dinner being prepared. It's really pretty. We relax on the terrace and soak up the surroundings, then go to take showers, rest, and write some cards home before dinner.

Now is a good time to get my Italian shower fixation off my chest. So far not one has had a glass door, and the plastic shower curtain provided always seems to gravitate to the body behind it. We are in fits of laughter later when we realize we have all been peeling plastic shower curtains from our bodies for a week. It's also a pity, we agree, that the funny long metal plugs with attached "controllers," provided for the washbasin, never stop the water from going down the drain—all of us are desperately trying to handwash because we still haven't found any kind of laundry service. And the bidets. Coming from a culture which doesn't use bidets, we have found them perfect for soaking the labels off wine bottles for Kevin to keep for future reference!

At dinner, Kevin chooses a local wine to start while we have his birthday presentation. I give him the two wonderful towels I purchased in Martina Franca, and he loves them. Sounds like a weird present, but Kevin and I always buy a set of towels when we travel. It's a nice way of remembering where you have been once you get home.

We taste two different wines with dinner—for research purposes only, of course. The guests, like the food, come from all over Europe—this place is a big contrast to where we were yesterday. The menu reflects the clientele more than it does the region, but the squid dish is outstanding.

After dinner we sit outside on the vine-covered terrace, with a canopy of shining stars above and the sea sparkling in the moonlight below. I think how wonderful it would be if everyone could see this part of the world, if only for a day.

Gail

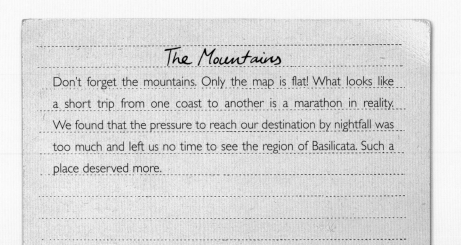

The Mountains

Don't forget the mountains. Only the map is flat! What looks like a short trip from one coast to another is a marathon in reality. We found that the pressure to reach our destination by nightfall was too much and left us no time to see the region of Basilicata. Such a place deserved more.

The town of Rivello clings to the side of a mountain in Basilicata

Pan-fried Squid with Herb Stuffing and Arugula Leaves

Calamari ripieni in padella

Serves 4

4 small squid (approximately 3 inches long)
2 tablespoons freshly chopped Italian parsley
1 teaspoon freshly chopped oregano
1 teaspoon chopped garlic
5 handfuls arugula
juice of 2 lemons
freshly ground black pepper
olive oil
4 anchovies
8 sage leaves
⅓ cup extra-virgin olive oil
salt

BEER BATTER
¼ cup cornstarch
½ cup all-purpose flour
¼–⅓ cup beer (lager or bitter)

1. Remove squid's head and eyes and reserve tentacles. Rinse interior cavity and remove thin filmy skin. Rinse and pat dry.
2. In a small bowl, combine parsley, oregano, garlic, 1 handful arugula, half the lemon juice, and a little pepper. Place about 1 teaspoon of this stuffing into each squid cavity. Chill.
3. To make batter, combine cornstarch with all-purpose flour and add beer, mixing to achieve pouring consistency. Season with salt and pass through a sieve to remove any lumps. Chill.
4. Lightly flour stuffed squid (not tentacles). Fry squid and tentacles quickly in a small amount of olive oil at a high temperature until golden brown on both sides. The tentacles should be crispy. Drain on paper towels and season with salt and pepper.
5. Sandwich each anchovy between 2 sage leaves. Dredge in flour and dip in chilled beer batter. Shallow-fry in olive oil until golden brown. Drain on paper towels.
6. Combine extra-virgin olive oil, remaining lemon juice, salt, and pepper to taste; toss remaining arugula with half this dressing.
7. Place some arugula in the center of each plate and arrange squid decoratively around. Garnish with an anchovy fritter. Drizzle remaining dressing over squid and serve immediately.

Highlights of the Day

Gail

Kevin

Simon

Robert

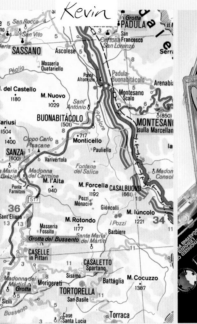

The Sea

Azure, aqua, midnight blue, jade, robin's-egg blue, opal, diamond, sapphire, emerald—the water is indescribable. By day, the sun creates a kaleidoscope of color. By night, the moon and stars glow over the water, making it velvety black and purple.

Driving Italian-style

I learned a few new lessons on the road from Monopoli to Maratea. On the autostrada, where speeds range from 60 mph in the driving lane to 95 mph in the passing lane, check your mirrors carefully before moving into the passing lane, or you could suddenly have a large Alfa Romeo touching bumpers with you. And take your sunglasses off in tunnels!

Tape Story

At the gas station, Gail and I decided we needed some Italian pop music for the journey. The attendant gladly gave us advice—this one was a local boy, that one a national hero, this one his favorite singer. Later we realized that he either had very bad taste in music or had off-loaded tapes he had been trying to sell for the last twenty years.

No Ordinary Gas Station

I was astonished to find that most large gas stations in this part of Italy also sell good food. Fresh, crusty bread rolls with mozzarella and prosciutto, beautiful salads with ripe tomatoes, baskets of delicious Italian sweets that we couldn't resist, and, of course, great coffee.

Wines of Puglia and Basilicata

Puglia produces a veritable flood of wine, making this the region with the largest wine output in all of Italy. For many years, the wines of Puglia were anonymously used for blending with the lighter wines of the north. This was largely due to the strength and structure of the wines, which achieve great ripeness and alcoholic strength from the fertile plains and scorching sun.

In the last two decades, however, a revolution has begun and it continues to gain momentum. Technology and a greater devotion to quality through modern growing and vinification methods have begun to mark Puglia as seriously competitive in the Italian wine scene.

Our education in the subject of Pugliese wines began with Daniele at Enoteca Massafra Daniele in Otranto. He guided us expertly through the local wine regions, highlighting the best wines in the provinces. I left his shop with a boxful of selections for us to sample over the next few days.

Puglia produces some of Italy's best rosé (*rosato*) styles, and we took the opportunity over lunch at Ristorante Da Sergio to taste the Rosato di Salento 1998 from Leone de Castris. Beautifully structured with an enchanting lightness and crisp finish, this wine enhanced our grilled seafood perfectly. Although we didn't have the opportunity to sample

the Salento Rosato "Five Roses," we were told that it is the pick of all the rosé wines available in Puglia.

After arriving at the Contento farm, I sorted through the day's purchases. The Locorotondo Bianco 1998 from Rivera would be sampled under the setting sun in the Contentos' walled garden, along with Salice Salentino Bianco 1998 from Francesco Candido. Both proved to be outstanding, with the Locorotondo exhibiting a dry softness with hints of hay and citrus. It coursed down our throats easily, being light in alcohol (11 percent) with a subtle acid finish. The Salice Salentino Bianco was also very good, charmingly fresh and fruity with a delightful balance.

On the morning of our second day at Curatori, I politely asked Signor Contento if I could provide a couple of bottles of wine for the next evening's dinner. I think he was interested, but pride would not let him acknowledge anything else but his own homemade wines.

That evening I presented two special bottles for his inspection—Patriglione 1993 from Cosimo Taurino and Castel del Monte Rosso Riserva "Il Falcone" 1995 from Rivera. As expected, I received a raised eyebrow and the question: "How much did you pay for these wines?" They were moderately expensive by Pugliese standards, both priced around $10 U.S. However, for premium wines of international standard, these prices were very reasonable.

The Patriglione is one of the signature wines of Cosimo Taurino. It is a blend of negroamaro and malvasia nera, harvested very late and at maximum ripeness. It is rich and powerful, yet with soft fruit and a velvety texture. The tannins provide subtle structure with acids to balance beautifully on the finish. Signor Contento and I nodded our approval.

The wine of the night was Il Falcone. It presents an intense bouquet of rich fruit and a palate that is dark and mysterious—a classic Italian red of powerful proportion followed by beautiful acid and length. This wine brought smiles to everyone's faces and proved to be the perfect accompaniment to Signora Contento's wonderful food.

Other wines to sample on your own visit to Puglia are Salice Salentino Rosso Riserva from Leone di Castris, one of the most famous full-bodied reds of the south, rich and powerful with full concentration and complexity. And if you can find it, the Donna Lisa Riserva will absolutely charm you.

For a variety of reasons, the region of Basilicata has had great difficulty in establishing itself as a serious player on the Italian wine scene. The area possesses great scenic beauty, with the right climatic, and geographic characteristics to become one of Italy's great wine regions. But an unfortunate reticence exists on the part of winemakers, possibly instigated by the inherent poverty of the area and the difficulty of using modern grape-growing techniques in such a harsh terrain.

The main wine-producing area is centered around Monte Vulture, an extinct volcano in the northern reaches of Basilicata. There are two wines which must be sought out, both from D'Angelo, located in the town of Rionero in Vulture. The white, Vigna dei Pini, is a blend of chardonnay and pinot blanc. The 1997 we drank is a truly elegant wine, nicely ripe with hints of flowers, fullish, but balanced with crisp acidity.

Aglianico del Vulture, the red, is the most famous wine of Basilicata. It is coarse when young and needs at least three years to be approachable; the Riserva is at least five years old on release. Our sampling of D'Angelo's 1995 Riserva showed a wine of deep intensity. It is powerful and evenly structured with hints of cherry and dark chocolate, and supple lingering tannins. Anyone interested in a great Italian red need go no further than this.

Kevin

Aglianico del Vulture is powerful and evenly structured with hints of cherry and dark chocolate, and supple lingering tannins. Anyone interested in a great Italian red need go no further than this.

Hac inscripno in epistylio inscuipta est,
neque votuit ob brevitatem fugli eo loco dimihi.

ghiera di ricambio

bruno   »   2.21

Vitello   » » » 1.20

Carne scelta » » » 1.55

senz' osso   » » » 1.95

Hac inscripno in epistylio inscuipta est,
neque votuit ob brevitatem fugli eo loco dimihi.

The Hills of Calabria

Friday, May 28

Life at the Villa Cheta Elite must be quiet—it's 7:30 a.m. and we are ready, but there are no other signs of movement. To be fair, they don't begin to serve until 8:00 a.m. In fact, no one has served coffee before that time on our whole journey.

Coffee and breakfast done, we are away to the mountains of Calabria for lunch. Two weeks before departing Australia we had no definite plans for this part of the Calabrian coast, on the "instep of the boot" from Maratea to Tropea. The towns here are all seaside resorts and most replied to our inquiries that they would be closed until June 1. So our travel agent, Judy Gillard, utilized the assistance of CIT, the Italian travel experts. On a visit to CIT's Melbourne office, Judy introduced us to Dawn and Aida, whom she hoped could help us with accommodation and places of interest in Calabria.

We met over coffee and Kevin spoke of his fascination for the hills of Calabria, with all the romantic stories of the Cosa Nostra hiding out there. We had found very limited tourist information for the south of Italy and wanted to know such things as what the regional food was like and details of local wine production. Dawn and Aida generously suggested that in Italy we should visit their families, who live in the area, for lunch on the way down to Tropea.

Within days it was organized; on the Friday we would go to Aida's cousin Domenico and his family for lunch, and on the Saturday we would meet Dawn's family.

So here we are, traveling south down the coast road and inland to Cervicati, the mountain town where Domenico lives. We pass through Scalea, where the coast is beautiful and ugly at the same time. The hills are wonderful, the sea is bluer than blue, but the holiday apartments and shops in between are an eyesore. I'm hoping Tropea, where we are staying for two days, is nicer than Scalea.

The Renault climbs up into the hills with no conception of what is ahead; we have no idea either. The road is steep. It tests Kevin's driving skills and our nerves as passengers. Halfway up we stop to ask directions, and the young man points to a road that seems to be hanging from the sky. I've been looking at it for ten minutes, quietly hoping it isn't the way to Cervicati.

The trip becomes completely beyond words. We are so high up—and the road is without guardrails. Kevin is driving and leaning away from the edge at the same time. At one point we stop to read the map and get out of the car for a stretch. I'm almost inclined to crawl on my hands and knees, it's so high. There is a little village on top of every hill. It's truly breathtaking and seems like we are hang gliding.

We are relieved to arrive, be it two hours late. Our hosts are the Monte family: Domenico and his wife Santina, Santina's Uncle Gino and his wife Mafalda, and Santina's father, Fiore Bosco. As we arrive in the town square, with a 360-degree view of what seems to be the rest of the world, Domenico is there to greet us along with half the town. They welcome us with open arms as though we are part of the family and from the moment we arrive it's noise, laughter, and food. Santina's 27-year-old niece Louisa, who lived in Manchester, England, until she was 11 years of age, is there to translate. She sounds completely charming, just like an Italian TV character.

These people are gorgeous. Santina, her aunt, and her sister-in-law tell us they have been cooking since early this morning. After experiencing the food that follows, I'd say the truth was that they had been preparing for a week.

The house, built on five levels, is lovely. There are two street levels and two kitchens. In the lower kitchen, the three women are in a frenzy of preparation. This working kitchen houses an open fire and a large oven, hotplates, and a sink. With all the food around them the cooks just fit. They show us three kinds of pasta they have prepared by hand for lunch—absolutely incredible. The upper kitchen is the show kitchen from where coffee and dessert will be served. The rest of the house is spacious, with the most beautiful marble floors. From the outside the house looks like one small part of a Lego Land of houses, but inside it is roomy, bright, and tasteful.

After much chatter we sit down for lunch. I count 35 different dishes, then stop counting. It is like going to a restaurant and ordering everything on the menu. The company is vibrant and with the help of Robert, Louisa, and Uncle Gino, the conversation flows beautifully. We are able to get a complete understanding of what we are eating and how it has been prepared. Robert and Kevin are writing frantically and our little tape recorders work overtime. I am sure Robert's version of this food will appear on the other side of the world on Donovans' table in the not-too-distant future.

There are the three pastas, soup, fried vegetables, fresh vegetables, involtini, homemade sausage and salami, eggplants cooked four ways, and figs cooked six ways, from sundried to wrapped in their leaves and cooked over the coals. The ten different cakes include little pastry pockets filled with dried seeded grapes and *bignè* with vanilla custard—a real highlight. The whole experience is a combination of culinary talent, generations of great tradition, and hearts the size of the mountains around us.

Trying to stand up after lunch is an effort. We join Domenico, Santina, and Louisa for a walk around the town. Only 600 people live here and most of them are aged between 50 and 90. The young people travel down the mountain daily to school and later leave the town for further study. There is a good hospitality college nearby due to the huge number of tourists who flock to the beaches along the coast, but sadly, the end result is that most young people need to leave the mountains for work. As Louisa explains, neither she nor her friends are interested in learning how to

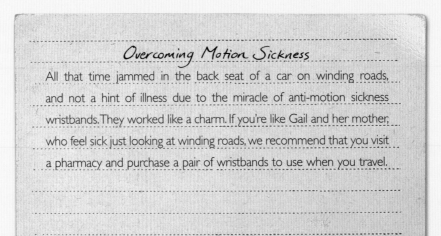

Overcoming Motion Sickness

All that time jammed in the back seat of a car on winding roads, and not a hint of illness due to the miracle of anti-motion sickness wristbands. They worked like a charm. If you're like Gail and her mother, who feel sick just looking at winding roads, we recommend that you visit a pharmacy and purchase a pair of wristbands to use when you travel.

cook or in living the mountain life. Understandable of course, but hopefully young families will eventually choose a quiet, healthy place such as this to raise their children, and the tradition will continue.

Our departure is much later than expected, with a few tears in the town square and all of us promising to visit each other as soon as we can. These people are like long-lost friends. Another unforgettable day—such generosity.

The return drive, down the other side of the mountain, is much quicker than the drive up, thanks to the autostrada. We are heading to the top of the toe for a couple of days by the sea. The good highway ends much too soon, and we spend a tedious two hours winding along the coast road through countless small, crowded towns on our way to Tropea.

We end up in the center of town at 8 p.m., in the middle of Friday-night traffic. I don't know how much busier it could be than this. We are all tired and full and I notice that Fangio has slowed down a lot and is letting everyone pass him. The tensions in the car mount; we're lost and impatient. I'm dreading finding the hotel—as most of Tropea is closed we have had to take a booking via the Internet for a hotel that none of the travel agents have ever heard of.

But suddenly things turn around. We find the hotel, Le Roccette Mare, and it is really superb, with large Mediterranean-style bungalows set on the sand and the old town of Tropea towering over our heads. At 9:30 p.m., just before the restaurant closes, we meet for a green salad and a well-earned glass of wine. Everyone is catatonic and we end up on the beach, throwing pebbles across the light of the water and splashing about with our pants rolled up.

Within seconds of going to bed there's a knock on our door and the waiter is there with my handbag, telling me I must be more careful. He's already visited Robert and then Simon looking for the owner. I can't believe, after telling everyone how dangerous it can be, that I left my bag at the table. No damage done, though: money, make-up, and mementos are all intact. The only thing damaged is my pride—I know I'm going to be the joke of the day tomorrow.

Gail

High in the hills of Calabria

Going to Mass in Cervicati

Lemon-scented Veal Meatballs

Polpette di vitello al limone

Meatballs have a long heritage in Italy, offering an inexpensive way of eating meat or using leftovers. This version has the piquancy of lemon, which considerably brightens the flavor.

Serves 4

1 slice white bread, crust removed
1 tablespoon milk
1 pound ground veal
1 clove garlic, crushed
2 tablespoons freshly chopped Italian parsley
zest of 1 lemon
¾ cup freshly grated pecorino romano
½ cup mortadella, finely diced
1 scant cup ham, finely diced
2 eggs
salt
freshly ground black pepper
12 lemon leaves
olive oil

1. Soak bread in milk for 5 minutes. Squeeze out excess milk and place bread in a bowl with veal. Add garlic, parsley, lemon zest, pecorino, mortadella, and ham. Crack eggs over mixture and combine thoroughly, using your hands. Season with salt and pepper.
2. Form mixture into 12 equal parts. Roll each piece into a ball between the palms of your hands. Flatten slightly to form an oval approximately 1 inch thick. Wrap a lemon leaf around each polpetto and fix with a toothpick. Chill for 1 hour.
3. Cook polpette for approximately 20 minutes on an outdoor barbecue, either on the griddle plate or over an open flame. Use moderate heat so as not to burn lemon leaves. Serve hot or at room temperature.

Fettuccine with Chickpeas and Chili Oil

Pasta con ceci

There are two versions of this dish: a soup with the addition of pasta or a pasta dish. Santina Monte's interpretation of the pasta dish was heightened with the addition of fiery chili oil.

2 cups dried chickpeas
water
6–8 cups chicken stock
4 cloves garlic, smashed
4 sprigs rosemary
3 bay leaves
½ cup canned seedless tomatoes, chopped
salt
⅓ cup extra-virgin olive oil
chili powder
1 pound good-quality fettuccine
freshly ground black pepper
freshly grated Parmigiano-Reggiano

1. Soak chickpeas in a generous amount of cold water overnight. Drain and discard soaking water.
2. Cover chickpeas with chicken stock, ensuring there is ample liquid to cover. Add garlic, rosemary, and bay leaves. Bring to a boil and reduce heat. Simmer until chickpeas are tender, approximately 1½ hours. Add tomatoes and simmer for 30 minutes.
3. Discard aromatics and season liberally with salt. Allow chickpeas to cool in cooking liquid. Drain and reserve liquid. (The result of the lengthy cooking time should be a significant reduction and concentration of the cooking liquid. The ideal result is a sauce-like ratio of chickpeas to liquid.)
4. Heat ⅓ cup of reserved cooking liquid with olive oil. Remove from heat and add chili powder to achieve a spicy oil.
5. Bring 5 quarts water to a boil with 4 tablespoons salt. Cook fettuccine until al dente and drain well, but do not rinse. Meanwhile, reheat chickpeas with remaining reserved cooking liquid. Return fettuccine to pot and toss with chickpeas and sauce. Season to taste.
6. Serve in shallow bowls, passing chili oil and grated cheese for your guests to add as they please.

Eggplant Croquettes with Tomato Sauce

Polpette di melanzane con pomodoro

There are a multitude of uses for the versatile eggplant in Italian cooking, with many recipes coming from southern Italy and Sicily. This version is our interpretation of a dish we enjoyed at lunch with the Monte family in the hills of Calabria. The eggplants are roasted over an open flame to impart a subtle, smoky flavor.

Serves 4

4 medium-sized eggplants
¼ cup sultanas
1 tablespoon finely chopped mint
2 tablespoons finely chopped Italian parsley
1 cup freshly grated pecorino romano
2 cloves garlic, minced
⅓ cup pine nuts
4 eggs
1 cup breadcrumbs
olive oil
salt
freshly ground black pepper

TOMATO SAUCE
⅓ cup olive oil
1 medium-sized onion, finely diced
2 cloves garlic, finely chopped
28 ounces canned, peeled Italian tomatoes with juice
12 basil leaves
pinch of sugar
salt
freshly ground black pepper

1. To make tomato sauce, heat olive oil in a saucepan. Add onion and garlic and fry until translucent. Add tomatoes and bring to a boil. Reduce heat and simmer for 30 minutes. Pass tomatoes through a food mill to remove seeds. Return to saucepan. Tear basil leaves into sauce, add sugar, and season. Simmer for 10 minutes and set aside.

2. Cook eggplants on a rack over an open flame. Turn frequently to ensure that all parts of the skin are blackened and the flesh becomes soft. Peel away skin, ensuring that all blackened pieces are removed. Rinse with cold water and pat dry.

3. Soak sultanas in warm water to cover for 10 minutes. Drain and chop coarsely. Preheat oven to 350°F.

4. Shred eggplant and then chop finely. Transfer to a mixing bowl. Add sultanas, mint, parsley, pecorino, garlic, and pine nuts with 3 eggs and ¾ cup breadcrumbs. Combine completely and season. The mixture should be moist and firm but not overly wet. More breadcrumbs may be added to bind the mixture further.

6. Shape mixture into 16 oval-shaped balls. Whisk remaining egg and dip polpette into it, coating completely. Dredge in remaining breadcrumbs.

7. Pour olive oil into a shallow frying pan to a depth of ¼ inch. Heat until oil is hot but not smoking. Fry polpette loosely, in batches if necessary. Turn to ensure they are golden brown all over. Drain on pape towels.

8. Transfer polpette to an ovenproof casserole. Add tomato sauce and bake, uncovered, for 20–30 minutes. Gently stir occasionally during cooking process.

9. Adjust seasoning and serve warm or at room temperature.

Poor Man's Bean Soup, Calabrian-style

Zuppa del povero

This is an excellent country-style soup. We love this style of cooking and the spirit of nurturing that it represents.

Serves 6–8

2 pounds dried cannellini beans
water
1 pound fresh borlotti (cranberry) beans
1 small bunch chard
3 stalks celery
1½ loaves casalinga bread, crusts removed
⅓ cup olive oil
4 carrots, cut into ¼-inch chunks
4 red onions, coarsely chopped
cloves from 1 head garlic, coarsely chopped
½ cup finely chopped Italian parsley
48 ounces canned Italian tomatoes with juice
9 ounces parmesan rind, cut into large chunks
salt
freshly ground black pepper
extra-virgin olive oil

1. Soak cannellini beans in cold water overnight. Remove any that have floated to the surface or are discolored. Drain and discard soaking liquid.
2. In separate pots, cover cannellini and borlotti beans with plenty of unsalted cold water. Bring to a boil and simmer until tender, approximately 45 minutes. Drain, reserving a few cups of cooking liquid.
3. Preheat oven to 350°F. Trim chard leaves and chop roughly. Run a vegetable peeler over backs of celery stalks to remove tough strings. Chop into ¼-inch chunks.
4. Cut bread into ½-inch chunks. Reserve one-third of chunks for garnish and soak the rest in 3–4 cups water until mixture has a porridge-like consistency.
5. Heat olive oil in a large ovenproof pot with a lid. Add chard, celery, carrot, onion, garlic, and parsley and cook over medium heat, covered, for 8–10 minutes, stirring occasionally.
6. Pass bread, tomatoes, and three-quarters of the cannellini beans through a food mill or sieve over the soup pot. Add remaining cannellini beans, borlotti beans, and parmesan rind with enough reserved bean cooking water to cover. Season to taste.
7. Bring to a boil, then cover and cook in oven for 2 hours, stirring occasionally.
8. Dry reserved chunks of casalinga bread in oven at 300°F for 10–15 minutes until crisp but not browned. Serve soup in bowls, garnished with casalinga chunks, and drizzled with extra-virgin olive oil.

Pastry Puffs with Vanilla Cream

Bignè

The Italian word bignè has been borrowed from the French beignet and is used to denote small puffs made from choux pastry and filled with cream. This was just one of the many desserts served at the Monte table for our lunch at Cervicati.

Makes 12

powdered sugar (optional)

Choux Pastry
1 cup water
½ cup unsalted butter, diced
1 tablespoon sugar
pinch of salt
1¾ cups all-purpose flour, sifted
5 eggs, lightly beaten
2–3 teaspoons vanilla extract
olive oil

Vanilla Cream
2 eggs
1 egg yolk
½ cup sugar
2 tablespoons cornstarch
2 cups milk
½ vanilla bean
zest of 1 lemon
1 tablespoon brandy
2 tablespoons unsalted butter, diced

1. Preheat oven to 400°F. To make pastry, combine water, butter, sugar, and salt in a saucepan and bring to a boil. When boiling point is reached, remove pan from heat and add flour all at once. Stir vigorously until mixture forms a ball.
2. Return pan to stove and "dry" paste over medium heat, stirring vigorously. This will take about 5 minutes. Paste is sufficiently dry when it comes away from sides of pan and there are tiny droplets of butter on its surface.
3. Remove from heat and add eggs 1 at a time. Stir rapidly, completely incorporating before next addition. Stir in vanilla extract.
4. Lightly oil a baking tray. Place mixture in a piping bag and pipe onto tray 12 balls 1–2 inches in diameter. Bake puffs for 20 minutes until golden brown and dry. Cool on a cake rack.
5. To make vanilla cream, combine eggs and yolk in a saucepan with half the sugar and beat together until mixture thickens slightly and is pale yellow in color. Mix in cornstarch. Remove from heat.
6. Place milk in another saucepan with vanilla bean, lemon zest, and remaining sugar. Heat to just below boiling point and then pour over egg mixture, whisking continuously. Add brandy and stir continuously over medium heat until mixture thickens and reaches a boil. Remove from heat and stir in butter. Strain mixture through a fine sieve. Cool.
7. Cut tops off puffs and spoon in vanilla cream until full. Alternatively, place cream in a piping bag, pierce 1 side of puffs and squirt in cream. Dust with powdered sugar to serve, if desired.

A memorable lunch with the Monte family in Cervicati

Highlights of the Day

Gail

Kevin

Simon

Robert

Déjà Vu

The closer we got to Sicily, the more I remembered about living there. The houses, the dark almond-eyed people, the little shops spilling out onto the streets. I couldn't wait to sit at my first lido in a deckchair, the sun on my face and my feet in the warm, clear blue water.

Polpette

Italians have a thousand ways in which to cook polpette, some with meat and others without. Whatever the composition, they are always highly flavored. An ancient recipe calls for the mixture to be shaped into "big mouthfuls." So that's how it got started!

Seeing Saints

After eating twice our capacity for lunch, we headed out for a look around the village. We stopped to admire the church, which seemed full to the brim with icons of saints. Surely there were more icons in the church than people in the town. The icons are all brought out and taken around the village once a week to serve and protect the people of Cervicati.

Tomatoes

It's hard to imagine Italian cookery without tomatoes. They actually originated in Mexico, but reached Italy in 1554 described as pomo d'oro — the golden apple. They were yellow, and no bigger than cherries. It took the Italians two centuries to learn how to eat them.

Swimming & Sunning – Stunning

Saturday, May 29

The orange juice served at breakfast is rich in color—not quite the bright red of the blood oranges of Sicily, but close—and bursting with flavor. We laugh constantly about me leaving my bag behind last night. Today we plan to drive back up into the mountains to meet Dawn's family, a long trip to what we expect will be another joyous, mammoth lunch.

We leave the hotel and the unthinkable happens; the Renault stops. Completely. Several phone calls later we have organized for it to be towed to a nearby garage for inspection and replaced if it can't be repaired. We phone Dawn's family to break the bad news to them, but the number we have is incorrect. It is such a disappointment—Dawn has been very helpful and we were so looking forward to another feast. We all feel guilty, but there is nothing we can do.

We regroup and decide that dinner will be at home tonight, as the apartment Kevin and I are in has a kitchen. Robert will be in charge of menu coordination. We climb the long, winding stairs from the hotel up the side of the mountain to the old town of Tropea. It is completely original and truly fascinating, with a view of the sea at the end of every small street. We feel at home with the healthy mix of tourists and locals.

A frenzy of food shopping begins as we shoot off excitedly in all directions to gather ingredients. The produce is plentiful and inexpensive, the shopkeepers patient and only too happy to provide tastes before purchase, with the result that enough food is purchased for a week.

At the Trattoria Tropea Vecchia, in the center of the old town, we have an hour-long lunch of the most perfect seafood pasta, spaghetti with clams, accompanied by home-made wine. Down the stairs to the hotel we go, laughing and with loads of shopping, as usual. We need several rest stops on the way, but it will be worth it to eat at our own table in peace tonight.

In the afternoon we take a rest—our first for days—in the lido attached to the hotel. I love lidos, those privately operated stretches of beach attached to hotels or roped-off sections of public beach. Here, for a minimal fee, you get your own little oasis with allocated deckchairs and umbrella and, of course, handsome, enthusiastic locals selling you everything from suntan lotion to beer, beach balls to fresh coconut and melon on ice. (As wonderful as lidos are, I do prefer our beaches at home, where the sand and sea belong to everyone.)

With several dips in the warm ocean, three hours pass like three minutes. Kevin and Robert are soon asleep and

We climb the long, winding stairs from the hotel up the side
original and truly fascinating, with a view of the sea at

of the mountain to the old town of Tropea. It is completely

the end of every small street.

Simon and I settle in for a good gossip about the people around us. Older Europeans obviously suffer none of the shyness about their bodies that we do—topless, G-strings, the lot, no matter what their age. Good for them, but it does take a bit of getting used to. There seem to be no worries about the sun and its effects on the skin here, either. Everyone is spraying oil on each other and baking. Simon and I are captivated by the local gigolos working the beach, targeting anyone young and female. Many of their advances are turned down, but some achieve success with their corny lines and persistence.

Tonight's meal will be a goodbye to Italy's "shoe," as tomorrow we make for the ferry to Sicily via Reggio di Calabria. Our whole journey revolves around eating—we are constantly looking at food or touching it, smelling it, or reading about it. No wonder every three or four hours we want to eat. Now, we start to look and chat seriously about ideas we have gathered that we might implement at Donovans. Simon has been shooting various ceilings, stone floors, food, and furniture for this purpose. How they might translate to our restaurant and party room in Melbourne remains to be seen.

Robert and I prepare dinner while Kevin and Simon choose from the box of assorted wines of Calabria that we have collected. The table is covered with food. The local salamis are wonderful, although the further south we get, the hotter the food is becoming. The bread has also been getting denser in texture and flavor. And the Calabrian cheeses—smoked provolone, pecorino, and mozzarella—are all delicious but very different in taste and texture to what we have previously eaten. There's also prosciutto and mortadella, fresh tomatoes, and quickly fried eggplant full of flavor, bottled local tuna drained of its oil and mixed with lemon and cracked pepper, the sweet purple onions of Tropea, and a delicious jar of onions and sultanas, almost like a chutney and very typical of the area. We eat the whole jar, mixing the contents with the other delicacies on the table and mopping up with fresh bread, and finish with tasty strawberries and cherries, at their best at this time of year.

Word arrives that the car has been fixed, which means we do not need to wait for a replacement vehicle. They will deliver it back in the morning, so there is no stopping us now. Sicily, here we come!

Gail

Travel Light

When going to Italy, don't pack too much. Cheap, cheery travelwear is everywhere. A week into our trip I had already sent back home more than half the clothes I had brought with me. Simon, a seasoned traveler, brought only what he was wearing, plus some T-shirts, socks, and undies. He was right!

Highlights of the Day

Gail

Kevin

Simon

Robert

Pottery Heaven

We just couldn't resist the ceramics in Tropea and ended up with presents, items for the restaurant, things we didn't need at all and two huge platters which became additional traveling companions for the following two weeks. I knew that once we got them home, they would be used and cherished always.

Tropea's Alimentari

Gourmet-style shops proliferate in the old town of Tropea. The typical Calabrian pork products are all on display, including tightly pressed soppressata, capocollo from the belly of the pig, and nduja, a pâté-like sausage that is very spicy. There are also many preserved sott'olio ("under oil") products, using the fine olive oil produced in the region.

Antique-hunting

When I enter a great antique shop I sense a certain smell, and then I go weak at the knees when confronted by the shop's treasures. I found such a place in Tropea. In the dim light beyond the vast terra-cotta oil jars at the entrance I could see carved marble and polished wood and old gilt. I was sure this shop would draw me back to Tropea some day.

Frutti di Mare

In Italy, shellfish are called frutti di mare—fruits of the sea. They are suited to Italian cooks, who love using fresh ingredients that are straightforward to prepare. Clams, shrimp, mussels, and scampi can be prepared simply by briefly steaming or frying, and flavoring with garlic, chili, parsley, and extra-virgin olive oil.

95

CIRÒ
DENOMINAZIONE DI ORIGINE CONTROLLATA

bianco 1997

Librandi

Wines of Calabria

For Calabria, like many of the regions of the south, most research gives the message that there are no great wines. This could not be further from the truth. While it is a fact that the north produces a greater proportion of fine wines and has better marketing, there are still many special wines in the south.

This is particularly true in Calabria, where we found a number of wines which we delightedly sampled on our balcony at Le Roccette Mare. Cirò Bianco is probably the most famous white wine of the region. The 1997 from Librandi is pale golden with soft acid and a hint of green olives. The other white, of slightly less prominence but no less quality, is Scavigna Pian delle Corte. We all agreed that the 1997 from Odoardi is a truly elegant wine with hints of dried herbs and citrus and a beautiful aroma of sea air.

There are a number of reds available. Try to find Gravello from Librandi, which is a blend of the traditional Calabrian red grape, gaglioppo, and the more familiar cabernet sauvignon. The result is a magnificent achievement, indicative of a great wine. The 1993 we drank is a dark, substantial wine with a flirtatious nose of spice and balsamic. It doesn't disappoint in the mouth, opening with great style and finishing with serious length. This is a true find.

The term *Classico* is used in Calabrian labeling and is attached to the red wine Cirò Rosso Classico Superiore Donna Madda. We tried the 1995, which has an intense and persistent nose and excites even more on the palate with soft, stylish emerging fruit.

A must-buy when in Calabria is the luscious, late-harvest wine called Greco di Bianco. You will find it only around Reggio di Calabria, where a few small producers make it their specialty. The finest, from Umberto Ceratti, is succulently sweet with orange-blossom tones and a satiny finish.

Kevin

for a week past and has been extremely
vain in showing the medal which they carry
as long as they continue at the top of the
class only. The rest are well in health
~~~~~~~~~~~~~~~~~~~~~~~ poorly in
~~~~~~~~~~~~~~~~~~~~~~~~ past with
~~~~~~~~~~~~~~~~~~~ She is however
~~~~~~~~~~~~~~~~~~ the last two
~~~~~~~~~~~~~~~~ a fair way
~~~~~~~~~~~~~~~ the cause of
~~~~~~~~~~~~~~ get sooner
~~~~~~~~~~~~ of egg cups
~~~~~~~~~~~ article for the
~~~~~~~~~~ and I hope you
~~~~~~~~~ pieces together
~~~~~~~~ way if you

~~~~~~~ nding to send
~~~~~~~ ipping but on
~~~~~~~ to his Aunt she found
she could not get it to send with the
Basket. She will have to send to Perth
next week and will write anent this
herself. Auntie Christy is so busy that
we very seldom see her — Tom says she

Heavenly Sicily

Sunday, May 30

We're up early for the big trip to Sicily. I'm so excited to be going back. Tropea feels a lot like Sicily, and yet not quite. We have decided to treat ourselves and celebrate our arrival by staying in one of the most beautiful hotels in Italy, way up on the hill of Taormina near where I used to live.

Our waiter at Tropea tells us we will never find our way to the autostrada. Never say never, but it does require much more time and energy than we expected. We stop several times to ask directions, as the road keeps winding through one small town after another. Every church is having Holy Communion. Girls in pretty white dresses and their overdressed, proud relatives are everywhere.

It takes two hours to reach the autostrada—we estimated half an hour—and the Italian drivers continue to flash by at incredible speeds. We wind our way down into Reggio di Calabria to catch the ferry, car and all. All four of us are concerned about this part of the trip because of the reputation that Calabria and Reggio have for violence and theft. It is unfounded. Poverty, yes, but we never feel remotely threatened.

We are on the ferry and off again at Messina before we know it. After 20 minutes' driving, Taormina begins to unfold its beauty with every turn of the road up the mountain. I feel as though I've never been here before as so much has changed, but somewhere inside me it feels very familiar. We arrive at San Domenico Palace Hotel way up on Monte Tauro by midafternoon, settle in, and begin to realize why we have come here. The hotel used to be an old monastery and is filled with exquisite antiques. At every turn there is an internal garden or a grand sitting room with beautiful terraces and views of the sea, with Mt. Etna looming over everything. It is truly stunning. The pool is spectacular, and the gardens are the best Simon has seen in his travels in Italy. None of us has ever seen anything quite like this place.

Over lunch at the pool, we soak up the atmosphere. The food is a wonderful surprise. We have the daily pasta of simple rigatoni with zucchini, antipasto of swordfish with a crisp fennel salad, fresh mozzarella, and tomatoes. I remember the taste of these rich, red tomatoes, grown in some of the driest and dustiest conditions in the world. To finish there is a radicchio salad, which we dress ourselves from the cruet set on the table, and an abundance of cold apricots, cherries, and loquats swimming in iced water. Home cooking is so unexpected in the environment of a grand hotel. We are presented with a huge piece of paper to sign, containing a scribbled list of what we have eaten. No prices. The "If you have to ask, you can't afford it" theory obviously applies here. We'll wait and see.

After a shower we head out into the streets. Taormina, Sunday afternoon! The town is a magnet for tourists and a chic and quite expensive place to stay. Everyone is out walking. Corso Umberto I is closed to traffic, so we don't need to fear for our lives as we wander and take in Sicily at its most luscious and sophisticated.

This street is famous for its food and wine stores. Wonderful cheese, pastries, marzipan fruits, exquisite wines, and unusual liqueurs are all here. The boys are so excited about what they have found that we decide on a picnic lunch tomorrow so that we can sample it all. I'm not sure how long I can keep eating like this, but so far all my clothes still fit when I breathe in.

Corso Umberto I also boasts some wonderful antique shops. You need to be careful though, as many of the items are highly priced copies. Trionfante Antichita, however, is a highlight, with medium-priced, genuinely old pieces.

Taormina's buildings are historic and in as immaculate a condition as I remember them. We come across lots of unusual stone floors, both inside buildings and out in the street. It will be interesting to see if we can find someone in Australia to recreate this look at Donovans without the hundreds of years of wear they have had here.

The late afternoon sun is brutal, and the many excellent gelato and cake shops have lines of people. We sample some miniature cannoli filled with chocolate custard as we head back to San Domenico, hot and tired, for a cooling dip in the pool and some relaxation.

Dinner is at a local restaurant, Ristorante al Duomo, said to specialize in Sicilian cuisine. It is a success, with good-quality food used in genuine local recipes. Sardines, capers, chili, swordfish, baby mussels, and clams—the food is definitely different in Sicily. Orange and lemon groves surround us on the hills; the smells, the wine, and even the bottled water have changed. That short ferry ride from Reggio di Calabria might just as well have taken us to another country. To some minds, Sicily is just that.

Before bed, Kevin and I sit on the huge terrace outside our room perched over the winding road below, looking at the sparkling lights of houses, hotels, and towns in the distance. The big, silver full moon creates a vibrant trail of light across the sea. Ah, the romance of heavenly Sicily.

Gail

Save Money on Accommodation

If you are on a budget, stay at the base of Monte Tauro in a city called Giardini-Naxos. It is less expensive and still lots of fun. Buses and cable cars run regularly to Taormina, so you can go up the mountain for the day and use the money you have saved on accommodations for shopping.

The beautiful gardens of San Domenico Palace

The locals describe Taormina as an island within an island the theater, mermaids splash in the sea below, and the swee

where the voices of ancient Greeks and Romans echo in life is lived in the cool, shady streets.

Fennel and Orange Salad

Insalata di finocchio e arancia

Sitting by the pool at the San Domenico Palace Hotel under the warm Sicilian sun, we were lucky enough to enjoy this salad with blood oranges. It doesn't get better than that.

Serves 4

6 blood oranges (or navels if blood oranges are not available)
1 bulb fennel, cleaned and trimmed
2 tablespoons finely diced fennel tops
⅓ cup coarsely chopped walnuts
5 tablespoons extra-virgin olive oil
sea salt
freshly ground black pepper
4–5 handfuls arugula

1. Peel oranges carefully, removing all of the white pith. Slice into ¼-inch rounds and remove seeds. Arrange orange slices in a shallow casserole dish just large enough to accommodate them.
2. Break off tender innermost leaves of fennel and slice into strips. Add to oranges. Sprinkle fennel tops and walnut over.
3. Pour olive oil evenly over salad and season. Refrigerate for 2 hours, basting several times to ensure flavors blend.
4. Wash arugula by soaking in cold water. Lift from water and pat dry. Refrigerate.
5. To assemble salad, transfer enough dressing from orange slices to arugula so that when tossed, leaves are barely coated and there is no excess dressing in bottom of bowl. Adjust seasoning. Arrange arugula on 4 chilled plates and top with the orange and fennel salad decoratively.

Spaghetti with Breadcrumbs

Pasta con la mollica

No one is really sure how breadcrumbs crept into southern Italian pasta dishes. One theory is that the people were too poor to use cheese and substituted toasted breadcrumbs. Whatever the story, their addition adds an interesting texture to a dish.

Serves 4

½ loaf stale casalinga bread
⅔ cup olive oil
3 cloves garlic, finely sliced
2 medium-sized onions, halved and sliced
1 dried bird's-eye chili, crumbled
28 ounces canned Italian tomatoes with juice
salt
freshly ground black pepper
5 quarts water
1 pound good-quality spaghetti *or* linguine
2 tablespoons freshly chopped Italian parsley
1 teaspoon freshly chopped oregano
2 tablespoons capers, rinsed and drained
½ cup black olives, stoned and cut into quarters

1. Grate bread to make approximately 1 cup crumbs. Heat 1 tablespoon of the olive oil in a skillet or frying pan. Add crumbs and stir repeatedly over medium–high heat until golden brown. Turn out onto a plate or baking tray to cool, stirring occasionally to stop cooking process.
2. In a shallow saucepan, heat remaining olive oil. Add garlic, onion, and chili and fry until onion is soft and translucent. Add tomatoes and simmer for 20 minutes. Adjust seasoning and remove from heat.
3. Bring water to a boil with 4 tablespoons salt. Add pasta and cook until al dente. Drain, reserving 1 cup cooking water. Do not rinse.
4. Reheat tomato sauce, adding reserved pasta water 1 tablespoon at a time to thin sauce to a consistency that will coat pasta evenly. Return pasta to cooking pot and add sauce. Add parsley, oregano, capers, and olives and toss to combine. Adjust seasoning.
5. Divide evenly among 4 plates and sprinkle with toasted breadcrumbs. Serve additional breadcrumbs on the side, if desired.

Pistachio Ice-cream

Gelato di pistachio

We enjoyed gelato in Rome and all over the south, but particularly in Sicily, where many will attest that the best is made. There can be much confusion over this Italian delicacy. In strict terms, gelato is an ice cream containing dairy and milk products. The icy version made from fruit, water, and sugar is sorbetto or granita.

Makes 1 quart

1 cup unsalted pistachio nuts, shelled
⅔ cup cream
⅔ cup milk
6 egg yolks
¼ cup sugar
pinch of salt
dash of kirsch liqueur
dash of vanilla extract

1. Preheat oven to 300°F. Toast pistachios until they begin to smell fragrant, approximately 10 minutes. Be careful they do not brown. Grind finely in a food processor.
2. Place cream, milk, and pistachios in a saucepan and bring to a boil. Remove from heat and steep for 20 minutes. Strain, discarding pistachios. Return milk to heat and warm to just below boiling point.
3. In a separate, medium-sized saucepan, mix egg yolks, sugar, and salt thoroughly, but do not whip or beat. Very slowly, pour hot pistachio milk on egg mixture, stirring well with a wooden spoon. A thick layer of foam will develop. Continue stirring over medium-high heat. As the custard heats further, the foam will disappear and the mixture will thicken enough to coat the back of a wooden spoon.
4. Remove custard from heat, strain, and whisk vigorously to stop cooking process. Cool. Stir in kirsch and vanilla extract and chill. Churn in an ice-cream machine according to the manufacturer's instructions.

Highlights of the Day

Gail

Kevin

Simon

Robert

Sleeping with a Monk

Often old buildings give me the creeps. Our room at the San Domenico Palace was large and grand with a terrace to match. However, I was sure I could hear chanting and the shuffle of leather sandals all night. If Kevin hadn't been by my side, I'd have been out of there. I don't sleep with monks.

Il Gelato a Passeggio

Literally translated, this means "taking the ice-cream for a walk." For the passeggiata, or evening promenade, the people of Taormina turned out to show off and look good, everyone sporting a cone or cup of colorful gelato. The locals were clustered around one shop in particular, La Gelateria on Corso Umberto I, where it is said the best is available.

San Domenico's Gardens

It was worth staying here just to see the brilliantly kept gardens hanging onto the side of the hill as if by a miracle. Cascades of bright bougainvillea, palms, large planted pots and jars, a cloister garden, and a citrus grove. What could be better than having a Campari at sunset in these gardens, with the smoking, active Mt. Etna as a backdrop?

Cannoli

Originally the culinary symbol of Sicily, these pastries are made by every bar and pasticceria in the south. In times past they were food for feast days and celebratory occasions. It was common practice to send presents to other families, and every time at least a dozen cannoli were sent.

107

The Heart of Taormina

Monday, May 31

Our five-star stay is over, with our next two nights booked at the two-star Villa Schuler, 100 yards below San Domenico. Our waiters at breakfast, served on the stunning San Domenico terrace, are friendly, seasoned performers. The breakfast buffet is huge—a hundred choices and all delicious. Between us we have a bit of everything, as usual.

We are permitted to leave our bags, but in the lobby, completely unprotected. I don't like the idea, but we leave them anyway and walk to Corso Umberto I. Shopaholics G. Donovan and Griffiths head off to buy clothes and shoes while the other Donovan and Robert go on a food and beverage excursion to purchase a picnic lunch, which we plan to have at the beautiful old Greek theater, about ten minutes' walk up the hill from the centre of Taormina.

We load the car and head down to Villa Schuler. Surprise, surprise! The owner is a gem and speaks perfect English. He helps us with everything, parks our car, and organizes a time to discuss where we should eat and advise us on our trip. We instantly feel at home in our large, charming rooms with an adjoining terrace overlooking the water. They have wonderful old furniture, cream damask floor-to-ceiling curtains and granite tiled floors. Later I see Mr. Schuler and his wife tending their lovely little garden and hanging out the guest towels to dry in the heat of the day. It reminds me of how Kevin and I work together in the restaurant trying to provide a special place and experience for our guests.

The Greek theater is like a mini-Colosseum perched on the hill. Despite its name, it was completely taken over by the Romans—and it shows. Rebuilt at the end of the first century A.D., it has arches, columns, dungeons, and an outstanding view of Mt. Etna (which Mr. Schuler has told us was erupting a week ago).

The picnic is a huge success, although a little hot. We are melting faster than the oven-roasted ricotta, and the prosciutto is curling. Deciding to go back to the hotel for a siesta, we have a wonderfully refreshing lemon granita on the way. Then another pottery shop, previously missed, pops up in front of us, so the shopaholics start all over again while the food and beverage department wanders home, too hot to wait.

Simon and I return to find Kevin reading on the terrace. We share our discovery of handmade soap, which we hope might make the harsh water a little kinder on our skin. Simon wants to get a haircut, so we go back out later to find the barber's shop we saw this morning, only to discover that every barber, hairdresser, and wigmaker is closed on

Monday afternoons. Instead, we walk right into a festival—"Mary, Helper of Christians." The bells are ringing, the local band is playing, and fireworks are set and ready to go. There are lines of young girls in beautiful white confirmation dresses, and the priest and his helpers in all their finery. And what would a festival in Italy be without the Virgin Mary? Here she is being paraded in the town square with at least twenty dozen roses bursting from around her feet and a halo made from flashing lights on her head. At last the people who live in the town are taking over from the tourists—and what an unexpected treat.

Later, back at the hotel, we drink Campari and soda and watch the bright orange sun sink into the blue, blue Strait of Messina. It seems so close you could touch it. The colors are like those chosen from a box of artist's crayons, too good to be true.

Dinner is at Ristorante Da Lorenzo, just around the corner, on the recommendation of Mr. Schuler. To get there we have to walk along a tiny mountain road. It's dark, the stone wall at the edge is low, and the drop is not worth thinking about. If one of the cars zooming past gets too close, the only way to go is over the edge. We are all wearing dark clothes, but somehow we survive.

We eat on the restaurant terrace, surrounded by a deep-purple bougainvillea hedge. This town is definitely the top end of the scale. The weather is made for outside dining—it's 86°F with not a breath of wind, a clear star-studded sky, and no flies. A huge black car pulls up and an older man in sunglasses and a woman get out, along with a man in a checked shirt and what looks like a hulky bodyguard. Convinced that the rugged man with the sunglasses is the Godfather, we sneakily take trips to the bathroom to look and report back. Sunglasses off, the man's real identity is exposed—it's movie-star time. It's Harvey Keitel, his wife, an interpreter, and a bodyguard. Now we know we are in the right place. We love a star!

The dinner is delicious: thickly sliced salmon, pasta with sardines and fennel, smoked swordfish, sea bass in its raw state under oil, good bread, and oven-smoked octopus. We select two large, fresh fish from the display—sea bass and big eye—to be roasted over the fire, meticulously boned, and served at the table with a green salad and roasted potatoes. The local wines are delicious—so much for the theory that real wine is only produced in the north. We continue to be captivated by the flavors and quality of both red and white wines.

People-watching is such fun. We monitor the slow decline of a super-groovy, designer-clad young Japanese couple as they consume too much wine and almost a bottle of grappa, which the waiter has continuously poured without them even noticing. Later, on the walk home, we see them leaning against each other at the edge of the town fountain, motionless, like two newly erected statues.

Safely back at Villa Schuler after a simply delicious meal, the moon is beaming across the water into our bedroom. What else is there for Kevin and me to do but sing a duet of "That's amore?"

Gail

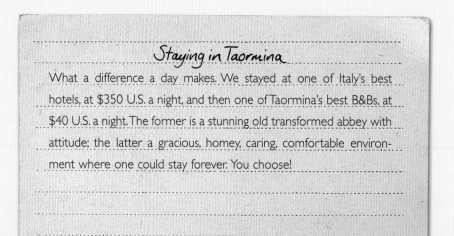

Staying in Taormina

What a difference a day makes. We stayed at one of Italy's best hotels, at $350 U.S. a night, and then one of Taormina's best B&Bs, at $40 U.S. a night. The former is a stunning old transformed abbey with attitude; the latter a gracious, homey, caring, comfortable environment where one could stay forever. You choose!

Picnic lunch at the
Greek theater in Taormina

VILLA
SCHULER

*Villa Schuler — a gracious, homey, caring, comfortable
environment where one could stay forever.*

Some of the lovely houses of Taormina

A tempting display of marzipan fruits

Bucatini with Sardines, Fennel and Breadcrumbs

Pasta con le sarde

This is the quintessential Sicilian pasta dish. It features some of Sicily's classic ingredients—wild fennel, which grows rampantly in the country-side, the freshest sardines just out of the water, saffron for a North African touch, and good pasta.

Serves 4

¼ cup sultanas
water
8 saffron threads *or* ½ teaspoon powdered saffron
salt
1 large bulb fennel with top, cleaned and trimmed
½ cup olive oil
2 onions, finely chopped
4 anchovies
2 pounds fresh sardine fillets, boned and cut into 1-inch pieces
¼ cup pine nuts
freshly ground black pepper
1 pound good-quality bucatini pasta
1 cup toasted breadcrumbs (see page 105)

1. Soften sultanas in lukewarm water to cover for 10 minutes. Drain and chop. Dissolve saffron in 2 tablespoons fresh water.
2. In a saucepan, bring to a boil enough abundantly salted water to cover fennel. Cook on a high simmer until tender, about 20 minutes. Drain, reserving cooking liquid. Press fennel with a fork in order to extract all liquid. Dice and set aside.
3. In a skillet or frying pan, heat olive oil and fry onion until just golden. Add anchovies and "melt" into onion. Add sardine pieces and cook over moderate heat for about 10 minutes.
4. Add diced fennel and simmer for a few minutes, then add pine nuts, sultanas, and saffron water. Adjust thickness of sauce with 1 cup reserved fennel water. Season with salt and pepper.
5. Pour remaining fennel water into a pot and add enough water to make 5 quarts. Add 4 tablespoons salt, bring to a boil and cook bucatini until al dente. Drain well, but do not rinse.
6. Reheat sauce and add bucatini, mixing well to blend flavors. Sprinkle liberally with toasted breadcrumbs and serve hot, warm or at room temperature.

Highlights of the Day

Gail

Kevin

Simon

Robert

Memories

*The next day we were due
to head down from Monte
Tauro to Giardini-Naxos,
the town directly below,
where I used to live. From
the top of the mountain, it
resembles New York with
its brightly lit buildings.
I was so glad to be in the
company of my darling
husband and two great
friends. Life in Giardini-
Naxos some twenty years
ago, as a stranger, had
often not been so
memorable.*

Sicilian Honey

The honey of Sicily is renowned
and considered to be energy
food because of its high sugar
concentration. The climate is
dry and constant without much
fluctuation in temperature or
rainfall, and no chemicals
or additives are used in
production. These factors, along
with very friendly beekeepers,
contribute to the excellence of
Sicilian honey.

Sweet Treats

*Robert and I took the
passeggiata in the early
evening and noticed the
incredible number of sweet
shops in Taormina. Their
lovingly crafted marzipan
displays featured fruit and
vegetables and miniatures
of fish, sausages, ham-
burgers, and fried eggs.
We stopped and bought a
bag of delicious pinoli
crescents, traditional
biscuits studded with
pine nuts.*

Santa Caterina d'Alessandria

This church has ages of history
all piled on top of one another.
It was built in the 1600–1700s,
but its foundations rest on a
Greek temple (500 B.C.), while
the buildings around the church,
only recently unearthed, date
from the 11th century. Taormina
at that time was an Arabic
center of commerce and
learning.

115

Taormina

Taormina 18/9 09

Aus Neapel zu Lande nach
Sizilien. Sie seht ihr unser
langer u. mühsamer (18ʰ bis)
hierher) Messina fuhr von
langer Entfernung aus
als ob nichts geschehen - in
der Nähe sieht man nur
noch die Hauptfacaden.
Fahren nun nach Palermo.
Es ist warm (ca 30° Schatten)
aber blau u herrlich schön
Herzlichsten Gruße an Euch u.
die Eurer

Karly

Signore
Josef Merz

Prokurist der Bank für Tirol

Austria, Innsbruck

Perlerstraße 9

Fishing for the Past

Tuesday, June 1

It's hot. Breakfast on the terrace is hot, our rooms are hot—it's definitely summer, and probably the very best time to be here before Taormina starts to burst with visitors. After breakfast Kevin and Robert meet an expert local chef in the garden for a chat, while Simon goes off bravely to have his hair cut. Probably for the first time since we left home, I'm alone. It's nice. I do the washing and sort the packing, which I have needed to do for days.

The chef, Biagio Lampo, is a friend of a friend of John Portelli, owner of an Italian import business in Melbourne. People in Italy always have friends or relatives in Australia—it makes the world much smaller. Robert, Kevin, and Simon are invited to the chef's restaurant, La Giara, at 5:00 p.m. to watch his kitchen preparation.

Back to the turmoil of driving up and down mountains. Kevin is certainly revitalized after a day without the challenge. We are off to Giardini-Naxos to see the town where I used to live. Initially I don't recognize anything, but as we approach the beach road certain things start to flash back.

Everyone is anxious to find my old house. After twenty minutes of walking and some assistance from the locals regarding directions we find ourselves drinking Sicilian beer with the people I used to live with—Giovanna and Giovanni Cirino. I had no intention of visiting them—I only wanted to see the house—but in my heart, encouraged by Kevin and Robert, I really needed to say hello, to thank them for looking after me. They are so happy to see me and say only gracious things about the time I spent there. My memory is that I wasn't always so gracious myself. I was continually frustrated by trying to understand a language dominated by local dialect and by striving to comprehend what was expected of a woman in a small town in Sicily in the 1970s. I never got the hang of either discipline.

The reunion over, we head for Castelmola, the small village on the mountain that towers over Taormina. In the piazza there is a beautiful bar with a fantastic view. Everyone loves it! For a surprise lunch I suggest the restaurant at Capotaormina, a large, modern hotel sunk into the side of the mountain. Entering this very 1970s hotel and seeing its staff dressed in corny, badly fitting national costumes, the boys aren't expecting anything special. We go through the lobby and down six floors; the elevator door opens onto a long, dark tunnel which winds its way to the sea. Simon thinks it looks like a scene from a James Bond movie. Eventually there is a ray of bright sunlight and the restaurant appears, cut into the rock on many levels. The ocean is 10 yards below, and there are pontoons and pool toys anchored to the rocks. It's a paradise of a place.

This restaurant was a permanent spot to visit when I lived here. My Dutch girlfriend at the time had a clothing shop too, and we would close at noon each day and go there for lunch and to sunbathe and swim. We were never hotel guests, but twenty years ago we were seen as tall, tanned, good-looking assets to have hanging around. What a laugh.

Lunch is a meal of help-yourself antipasto, fresh fish grilled over a charcoal fire, and fabulous fruit of vibrant pinks and oranges such as only a harsh, dry place like Sicily can grow. We had planned to take the cable car down to the lido at Mazzarò for an afternoon swim, but time has flown and the men need to keep their appointment with the chef in Taormina.

Peaceful again, I stay at Villa Schuler completely content to organize a few things for tomorrow, when we will be on the move big-time. Later I sit on the terrace, watching Mt. Etna drifting smoke across the sky.

The crew arrives back from the restaurant after cooking lessons using local cuisine—gnocchi made with fresh ricotta, and everything about swordfish they thought they knew, but didn't. This is information from a different level, through the eyes of a master chef rather than a cook in a home kitchen—although neither is better than the other. Northern Italians would argue that in the south it doesn't matter who cooks because theirs is the only kitchen. I beg to differ, but that's another story.

Dinner has once again been organized by our host. I think Mr. Schuler is the most organized person in Italy—

a truly great hotelier. Our request for dinner was to eat by the water, a typical tourist wish. He arranges for a taxi to take us to Letojanni, the next town to Giardini-Naxos. Ristorante Da Nino is a bit rough and ready, with plastic chairs and unshaven owners with attitude, but we could not have dreamed of a more perfect place to eat.

While we order wine, a local fisherman arrives with his catch still wriggling. We begin with a plate of fried whitebait followed by simply boiled baby shrimp. The idea here is to just pop off the head and eat the rest—legs, tail, and all. They disappear from the plate in seconds. Next are mussels quickly steamed in their own juices with a dash of wine, opening and spilling their flavors into the broth, and mussels baked with breadcrumbs and a little chili. The steamed version is a taste of the sea of Sicily, and very addictive. They are so good we order another plate!

Spaghetti with clams is next, followed by homemade *maccheroni alla Norma* with fresh tomato and eggplant. Robert is raving about it. The flavor of the sauce is intense and a new taste for us all. Perfectly grilled large red shrimp, swordfish, and more shrimp in light tomato sauce follow. To finish there is coffee, with toffee-dipped almonds and biscuits rolled in pistachios. Delicious!

Add in the sand, a full moon over the water, and the silhouettes of small fishing boats bobbing up and down, and I can think of no better way to say goodbye to the place I have dreamed of seeing for so long.

Gail

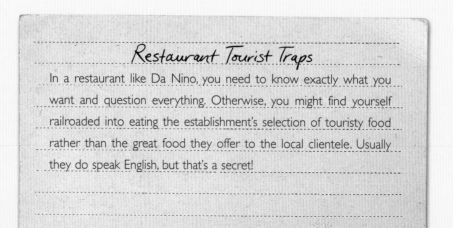

Restaurant Tourist Traps

In a restaurant like Da Nino, you need to know exactly what you want and question everything. Otherwise, you might find yourself railroaded into eating the establishment's selection of touristy food rather than the great food they offer to the local clientele. Usually they do speak English, but that's a secret!

Shaved Swordfish with Olive Oil and Blood Orange Juice

Pesce spada con olio e arancia sanguigna

Swordfish is prized all over Sicily, but particularly along the Strait of Messina. The most popular preparation is involtini, where the fish are rolled in breadcrumbs and baked. We prefer the simpler preparations, especially when the fish is extremely fresh. In this recipe, the acid in the blood orange juice gives a "cooked" texture to the fish.

Serves 4

1 × 17-ounce swordfish fillet
juice of 1 blood orange
1 clove garlic, crushed
⅓ cup extra-virgin olive oil
½ medium-sized onion, very finely chopped
2 tablespoons freshly chopped Italian parsley
sea salt
freshly ground black pepper

1. Chill swordfish well to make it easier to slice. Slice as thinly as you can, approximately ⅛ inch per slice.
2. Squeeze half the orange juice over fish, turning slices to ensure they are evenly coated. Add garlic and refrigerate for 2 hours, covered, turning occasionally to ensure garlic and orange flavors are evenly distributed.
3. When ready to serve, drain off juice and discard garlic. Transfer swordfish slices to a decorative serving platter and dress with olive oil and remaining orange juice. Sprinkle onion and parsley over and season with salt and pepper.

A welcome-back from Giovanna and Giovanni in Giardini-Naxos

View from Capotaormina

Whole Fish on the Barbecue

The objective in grilling fish is
to cook quickly over very hot
coals. Ideally choose fish
that are firm in texture
to handle the intensity
of the heat from the grill.

Chef Biagio Lampo makes gnocchi at his restaurant in Taormina

Ricotta Dumplings with Tomato Sauce

Gnocchi di ricotta con pomodoro

There are many versions of these dumplings in Italian cooking and each region claims to have the best recipe. Although it is not strictly a dish of the south, chef Biagio Lampo prepared this recipe at his Taormina restaurant before the evening's service.

Serves 4

9 ounces ricotta
1½ cups freshly grated pecorino romano
1 egg
pinch of nutmeg
1 cup all-purpose flour
salt
3 quarts water
1 quantity Tomato Sauce (see page 82)
2 tablespoons freshly chopped Italian parsley
freshly grated Parmigiano-Reggiano

1. In a bowl, combine ricotta, pecorino, egg, nutmeg, and half the flour. Add salt to taste and mix to create a dough-like consistency. Add remaining flour and mix to make a stiff dough.
2. On a lightly floured surface, form mixture with palms of your hands into 6 cylinders approximately 1 foot long and ½ inch in diameter. Cut each cylinder into ¾-inch pieces and press lightly with the back of a fork, pulling fork towards you. This will create the traditional "ribbing" necessary to trap sauce.
3. Lightly salt water and bring to a boil. Cook dumplings in batches. When they rise to the surface after about 2 minutes, remove with a perforated spoon to a skillet or frying pan and keep warm. Repeat until all dumplings are cooked.
4. Warm tomato sauce and pour over gnocchi. Simmer until just warm. Scatter with parsley and serve with Parmigiano-Reggiano.

Fried Whitebait

Merluzzo fritto

*These tiny fish, only 1–2 inches long, can be eaten whole because their
internal bone structure is so delicate. At Ristorante Da Nino we were
treated to tiny cod which were at the pinnacle of freshness and
beautifully crisp when cooked.*

Serves 4

1½ cups all-purpose flour
salt
¼–½ teaspoon cayenne pepper
1 pound fresh *or* frozen whitebait
olive oil
2 cloves garlic, squashed
lemon wedges

1. Season flour liberally with salt and cayenne pepper. Pat
   whitebait dry with paper towel and flour quickly, tossing to
   ensure they are evenly coated. Place in a fine mesh strainer
   and sieve away excess flour.
2. Pour olive oil into a skillet or frying pan to a depth of 1 inch.
   Warm oil with garlic until hot but not smoking. Remove garlic
   when it begins to brown.
3. Pan-fry whitebait in batches until golden and crispy. Drain on
   crumpled paper towels and serve immediately with plenty of
   lemon.

Macaroni in the Style of "Norma"

Maccheroni alla Norma

Serves 4

salt
2 medium-sized eggplants, cut into ¼–½ inch slices
½ cup olive oil
1 zucchini, finely chopped
1 red pepper, finely chopped
2 cloves garlic, finely minced
14 ounces canned, peeled Italian tomatoes with juice
2 tablespoons tomato paste
16 basil leaves
freshly ground black pepper
5 quarts water
1 pound good-quality macaroni or rigatoni
dry ricotta, grated

1. Salt eggplant slices liberally and allow to stand for 1 hour. Rinse and pat dry. Fry in ¼ cup olive oil on both sides until golden brown. Drain on paper towel.
2. Pound zucchini and red pepper in a mortar and pestle until a paste is achieved.
3. In a skillet or frying pan, fry garlic in remaining olive oil until just colored. Add zucchini and red pepper paste and cook for 2 minutes. Add tomatoes and tomato paste and simmer for 30 minutes.
4. Tear half the basil leaves into sauce and season with salt and pepper. Stir in eggplant.
5. In a large pot, bring water to a boil with 4 tablespoons salt. Cook macaroni until al dente. Drain well, but do not rinse. Return macaroni to cooking pot and add sauce. Stir to combine, adjusting seasoning.
6. Tear remaining basil leaves over and serve with plenty of grated ricotta.

Almond Kisses

Bocconetti di mandorla

Our memorable dinner at Ristorante Da Nino finished with these little confections.

Makes 3 dozen "mouthfuls"

2 tablespoons butter
2 tablespoons flour
3 cups blanched almonds
2 cups sugar
½ teaspoon vanilla extract
3 egg whites
jam *or* preserves of your choice
powdered sugar (optional)

1. Preheat oven to 350°F. Butter 2 cookie sheets and sprinkle with flour, tapping to ensure whole sheet is coated. Shake off excess flour.
2. Grind almonds to a fine meal in a food processor or nut grinder. Stir in sugar and vanilla extract.
3. Beat egg whites until soft peaks form. Fold in almond mixture, mixing well to form a workable paste.
4. Shape 1 tablespoon of mixture into a ball about 1 inch in diameter. Poke a hole in the center and fill with ½ teaspoon of jam. Cover hole with a small amount of almond mixture and roll gently between palms of your hands until ball is well sealed. Repeat with remaining almond mixture.
5. Bake for about 25 minutes until delicately browned. Cool on wire racks. Sprinkle with powdered sugar, if desired. Almond kisses will keep for 3 days in an airtight container.

Highlights of the Day

Gail

Kevin

Simon

Robert

On Top of the World

Castelmola is blessed with a glorious view and a great coffee bar. At certain times of the year it becomes a festival town and the funny costume-covered horses and carts sold in every souvenir shop come to life. If you ever go to Taormina, don't miss Castelmola— it's like being on top of the world.

Granita with Fresh Strawberries

Gerhard Schuler appeared on the terrace bearing a tray of glasses of fresh strawberry granita. We will remember this season's first crop of strawberries for their delicious full flavor and for Mr. Schuler's deft technique at preparing one of Sicily's age-old delicacies.

Encounter with Fame II

At Capotaormina I took a few general shots of the restaurant. A burly American inquired a little too intently whether I had taken his friend's picture or just the view. He asked me to shake my head so his friend could see my reply. Mr. Burly walked off, and I realized he was the bodyguard from the night before when I saw him sit down at a table nearby with Harvey Keitel!

Maccheroni alla Norma

The wonderful pasta dish we enjoyed at Ristorante Da Nino originally came from Catania. It is so named after the opera "Norma" by Bellini. The people of Catania consider this work an operatic masterpiece, and translated its name to this culinary masterpiece.

The Aeolian Islands

Wednesday, June 2

We load the car early and say a heartfelt thank-you to Gerhard and his Villa Schuler, then head north back to Messina for our journey to the Aeolian islands of Lípari and Salina. Driving out of Taormina and onto the autostrada, it's in and out of the never-ending tunnels and over the countless bridges once more.

Then the inevitable happens—a truck traveling eight or nine cars in front of us swerves and tips over. Luckily no one is hurt, but the upturned truck completely blocks both lanes. All the traffic around us comes to a screaming halt in a dark tunnel full of fumes, and after just a few minutes a police car miraculously weaves its way through to the scene of the accident.

We do what everyone else does—get out of the car and walk to the end of the tunnel to get some fresh air and pass judgment on the situation. It's incredibly smelly outside the car, but how often do you get the opportunity to walk through an Italian autostrada tunnel?

Apparently the truck cannot be moved without a crane. We calmly accept that we will be stuck for some time, but the problem is solved surprisingly quickly and efficiently. Within half an hour the road is clear and we are on our way once more.

With our luggage and car safely stowed at a hotel in Milazzo to be collected when we return from the islands tomorrow, we take a cab to the port. The hydrofoil arrives promptly, and we are off to Lípari, standing outside on the deck for a view of the islands. It is hot inside the cabin, and Kevin is the only one of us who is not susceptible to seasickness. I'm glad to disembark. It is busy, and we are running late for our lunch booking at the famous Filippino restaurant up the hill from the port. We have read a lot about this place, but it turns out that our expectations were too high. They are not at their best today; in fact, they are not interested in looking after us at all. Very disappointing!

After lunch we walk through the lovely little streets to see what we can of the town before getting back on the boat to Santa Marina di Salina. Lípari's port truly reflects the nature of the island. Children use the jetty as their playground, fishing and digging in the sand oblivious to the tourists. Some of the more enterprising kids sell shells and pumice stones from little stalls they have set up. There is no threat of danger here, just healthy daily life on a dreamy island, visitors welcome.

I really like these islands. Salina turns out to be even more isolated and quaint than Lípari. Its friendly, gracious people are anxious to assist and eager to share their hometown with visitors. We stroll from the port to meet Antonello, the driver of what must be the oldest tourist minibus in the world. He drops us at our hotel, Mamma Santina, and we arrange for him to collect us again at 8:30 p.m. for a trip around the island. The pensione is perfectly situated and looks beautiful, although it's by no means lavish.

Salina is a special place for Robert. He's been quiet and preoccupied all day. This is where his mother was born, and I know he's anxious to visit the house where she lived as a child, even if it has fallen down. He heads off and the rest of us go to the beach for a swim. The sand is as black as can be from the nearby volcano, and the rocks are brutally sharp—now we understand why all the guidebooks tell you to wear plastic shoes when you swim here. I can't imagine what we look like, wobbling and staggering over the torturous rocks to get to the water!

We meet for a late dinner prepared by Mario Gullo, the young man who owns the pensione. Robert shows us an old tile he found at his mother's house. It's beautiful and I'm sure it will be treasured by his family. He reminisces about his mother's cooking, describing in detail her *caponata* (sweet-and-sour eggplant) and very special fish soup.

Mario prepares an excellent dinner for us—good local produce beautifully cooked and served with a smile. It includes some of his mother's special recipes and the flavors are explosive. Dried tuna, a salad of wonderful greens with capers, and spaghetti with a sauce that looks like deep-green pesto but has tastes of chili, capers, and oregano. The *caponata* is also a sensation.

The real fun on this breathless, balmy night begins when we retire to our patio after dinner to play the Sicilian card game called *briscola*. Simon has been driving Robert nuts for a week to teach him how to play. Featuring every Italian swear word I've ever heard, the game is lots of fun and continues late into the night with the players showing more and more bravado as the wine flows like water. Robert beats us all, easily.

Gail

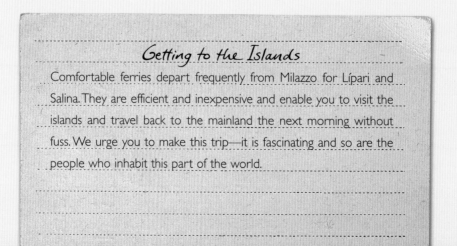

Getting to the Islands

Comfortable ferries depart frequently from Milazzo for Lípari and Salina. They are efficient and inexpensive and enable you to visit the islands and travel back to the mainland the next morning without fuss. We urge you to make this trip—it is fascinating and so are the people who inhabit this part of the world.

o è andata sempre
il bisogno d'espa
alia, prima della
e in Africa: l'Eri
ia, sulla costa dell
Turchia in seguito
editerraneo.

1. Having obtained
into the solution o
nment had left the co
articularly the case
ll [1] faith in the justic
vate vengeance. 5.
in proportion to it.[2]
ary that these co
d everywhere. 8. F
s was adopted for a
e to improve the eco
ry.

1. Having transferred the capital to (in) the Eternal City
government started
ult to solve all the
s. 3. But the need
n statesmen. 4. In
ous progress. 5. I
the economic condi
oday Genoa is the b
n and Milan are an
pe. 7. Italy's popu
reds of thousands o
n countries. 8. Ha
ly distinguish thems
re glad to see them
tion to our material.

¹ Ogni.

(rimanere) Esse non ——
are il miglior posto.
(rimanere) Gli zii ——.
ini nel cassettone.
3. *(rimanere)* Voi
quello spettacolo? 6. *(dovere)* I miei
Essi —— andare alla
inerica. 9. *(vedere)*
vermi spesso?

ustria si ebbero in
i ribellarono ai loro
onte con plebisciti
1860. Napoleone
ifestazione del voto
tenne dal Piemonte,

ò la conquista del
aribaldi. Giuseppe
s'era arrolato tra i
era già coperto di
oma e nella recente
Alpi, concepì l'idea
dei Borboni.
i su due piroscafi, e
ve la popolazione lo
L'impresa sembrava
italiana per cui quei
tutta la Sicilia fu-
ccorrevano volontari
ective of their ending.

Maria's Fish Stew

Zuppa di pesce di Maria

Robert says he can still remember his mother's fish stew, lusty with the scent of fresh garlic. Be sure to get a good mix of fish and cook each variety only until it is done. Do not overcook.

Serves 6–8

6–7 pounds assorted whole fish (such as cod, whiting, John
   Dory, snapper, trout, etc.), cleaned and scaled
9 ounces mussels, scrubbed
9 ounces clams, scrubbed
1½ cups dry white wine
2 bird's-eye chilies
olive oil
2 large onions, finely chopped
5 cloves garlic, finely chopped
28 ounces canned, peeled Italian tomatoes with juice
¼ cup red-wine vinegar
salt
freshly ground black pepper
9 ounces shrimp in their shells, heads on
6–8 slices casalinga bread

1. Chop some of the fish into chunks, leaving the bones in, and fillet others. Reserve 3–4 fish heads.
2. Steam mussels and clams in half the wine until just opened. Transfer to a bowl and set aside until required. Reserve cooking liquid.
3. Finely slice chilies, reserving seeds. In a large casserole, heat ⅔ cup olive oil and fry onion, garlic, and chili (slices and seeds) until light golden. Add fish heads and tomatoes and simmer for 15 minutes. Remove fish heads and discard.
4. Add remaining wine, reserved shellfish cooking liquid, and red-wine vinegar, and simmer for 15 minutes. Season.
5. Add firmer-fleshed fish, large pieces first. After 3–4 minutes add fillets and more delicate fish. After another 3–4 minutes, add shrimp. A minute or two later, add mussels and clams and simmer just long enough to warm them. Adjust seasoning.
6. Brush bread with a little olive oil and toast under an oven griller until golden brown. Warm serving bowls and place 1 slice of toast in each. Ladle fish stew over and serve.

Sweet-and-sour Eggplant

Caponata

This is a staple of the Italian antipasto table. Make it in large quantities—it keeps for several days and improves as the flavors marinate.

Makes approximately 1½–2 pounds

3 medium-sized eggplants, cut into ½-inch cubes
salt
olive oil
heart from 1 bunch celery, finely chopped
2 medium-sized onions, halved and sliced
16 ounces canned Italian tomatoes (peeled, seeded) with juice
freshly ground black pepper
½ cup red-wine vinegar
1 tablespoon sugar
⅓ cup green olives, quartered
½ cup capers
hard-boiled eggs, cut into quarters (optional)

1. Salt eggplant cubes and place in a colander for 1 hour, weighted, to extract juices. Squeeze and pat dry. Do not rinse off salt.
2. Pan-fry eggplant in olive oil over medium heat in batches until golden brown on all sides. Drain on paper towels. In the same oil, fry celery until golden. Drain on paper towels.
3. Wipe out pan and heat 4–5 tablespoons fresh oil. Fry onion until golden. Add tomatoes and season with salt and pepper. Simmer for 15 minutes.
4. In another pan, heat vinegar and dissolve sugar in it. Marinate olives and capers in this mixture for 15 minutes.
5. Mix eggplant, celery, and onion and tomato mixture into marinade. Simmer for 15–20 minutes until eggplant is very tender.
6. Let flavors blend for a few hours or overnight. Serve chilled or at room temperature. Garnish with hard-boiled eggs, if desired.

Highlights of the Day

Gail

Heart and Home

After World War II many people left Salina for other countries, especially Australia and America. Some never returned; others came back many years later to find they now felt at home in neither country. Today the locals send their children away to be educated abroad, and it seems inevitable that, like their forebears, they will forever be torn between the old and the new.

Kevin

Dinner at Mamma Santina

The highlight of our dinner was the spaghetti with caper pesto. Mario told us that the recipe has been handed down through generations of mothers in his family. It contains thirteen special ingredients, and he challenged us to name them all. We identified only nine, thus leaving the secret safe for another generation.

Simon

Briscola

On the way to catch the ferry to Lipari we saw Milazzo's fishermen selling their morning's catch. A group of old salts were playing cards, which reminded me that Robert had promised to teach us the Italian game of skill, cunning, and bluff called briscola. After one short lesson we were all hooked.

Robert

Capers

Famous throughout the world, the capers of Salina love the heat and flourish in the volcanic soil. They are sun-dried and then cured with sea salt in wooden barrels. My mother's family were employed as caper pickers and used to go out at first light to work until noon, when the sun would get too hot for them to continue picking.

135

High & Dry

Thursday 3 June

An early wake-up call. There's no need for me to go over the story of Italian plumbing and plastic shower curtains again here—suffice to say that this bathroom, which we are all sharing, takes the cake. One shower and it instantly turns into a lake. Add a bit of black sand from yesterday's trip to the beach and it's like a big mud pie.

Antonello, the driver we booked to take us around the island, doesn't arrive. We walk down to the port and find him in the local bar. All he says is "Are you ready?" It's an Italian thing—Robert knew he would be there.

It is very, very hot. There are five of us and all our bags in a tiny van that hasn't had shock absorbers for years. It's quite comical as the van struggles to make it up the steep roads—we could walk faster! Antonello is delightful and takes us via the scenic route to the Hauner winery, which Kevin has been looking forward to visiting for days. We sample red and white wines, grappa, and the famous dessert wine, Malvasia delle Lipari. The winery also produces vegetables *sott'olio* and beautiful local salted capers.

We have had enough of the sardine can on wheels; there isn't time to tour the whole island and we have a long journey ahead, so we decide to depart Salina early. We take the ferry back to Milazzo, collect our luggage and the car and by 1:00 p.m. are traveling west into the mountains.

We turn off to the small town of Pettineo and get lost again. After four stops to ask for directions, we find the place we are looking for. The family of our hosts, Maria Teresa and Sebastiano Allegra, has owned Casa Migliaca for over 200 years. It is a beautiful, sandstone-colored, double-story house surrounded by palms, olive trees, lush green mulberry trees, bright pink oleander, and succulent cactus. This agritourism farm is rustic but incredibly stylish. Robert and Simon think it looks like Tuscany without the cypress trees, and with the addition of some very, very high mountains.

The house is in immaculate condition. It has always had people living in it and has never been allowed to slip into a state of disrepair. The old working kitchen upstairs and the guest rooms are magnificent—Maria Teresa and her husband have the ultimate good taste. There are white linen curtains, whitewashed walls and original tiles in each room, and the bed linen has wooden buttons and hand-stitched buttonholes. The detail, whether original or not, is completely in keeping with the character of the house.

We spend the late afternoon out in the garden wandering, writing, and assisting Simon with his photography. He and Robert love it here, but I have to admit that Kevin and I are a bit sick of minimal amenities and roughing it. I want to be comfortably cool, but I'm not. I want to love the toilet and shower in a space the size of a broom closet, but I don't. I want not to mind being eaten alive by mosquitoes and looking as if I've been attacked by Dracula, but I can't.

Back to the romance. We sit in the garden eating fresh green almonds straight from the tree with the "Queen's biscuits," sipping Malvasia delle Lipari. A great combination.

At dinner we take our places around the original olive oil press, now a huge stone table. In the center is the biggest "lazy Susan" I've ever seen, for moving the food around. Our hosts join us along with their son, his friend, two artists from Germany, and two doctors from Messina, making a table of twelve. The women who cook at these agritourism farms are heroes. All day, every day they cook, and every night they play hostess to the world and share their table. This meal is nothing short of a miracle, with the food prepared by Maria Teresa in the beautiful old kitchen on the floor above and passed down a tiny ladder to the table.

There's pasta with zucchini, two ways. The first is macaroni served with a sauce made from herbs and the leaves of the zucchini plant; the second is tiny penne with the fruit of the zucchini plant, with beautiful local pecorino grated on top. Imagine the variety of flavors and textures in these incredible dishes, both of them driven by the need to find a way to utilize every possible growing thing this dry landscape can produce.

The lazy Susan continues to swing by, loaded with wonderful homegrown olives, grilled eggplant, slices of roasted squash with mint, chilled poached veal with citron, and meatballs with pesto, to match potato salad with virgin olive oil, capers, and basil, and a green salad garnished with boiled lemon pieces and green beans and onions. It keeps turning and turning in front of our faces, the central plates emptying one by one, until everything on it has been consumed with relish and delight. We finish with Sicily's unparalleled fresh fruit and a large, citrus-flavored, fish-shaped gelatin mold, translated for us as "jellyfish."

In our shared apartment next to the dining room, Kevin and I take the room where the good old donkey used to sleep after hours of walking around in circles propelling the stone wheel to crush the olives. Simon and Robert share the Gold Room, where the first press of the olive oil was stored many years ago. The mosquitoes descend and I cover my head with the sheet, scratching like a dog without a flea collar. Then I sleep. *Gail*

Changing Traveler's Checks

Don't frustrate yourself by trying to change traveler's checks in small towns that don't see a lot of tourists. Traveler's checks are supposed to be like cash, but you can't tell that to small local banks. Change your checks in large towns and stow the cash in your money belt. You'll save hours of time.

Casa Migliaca

Enjoying the hospitality of Maria Teresa and Sebastiano at their farmhouse

Fresh Almonds with Cheese

There is no greater delicacy than sweet almonds picked from the tree when they are perfectly ripe. Peeling back their green shell reveals a tender and juicy centre. They were the perfect accompaniment to the fresh cow's milk cheese of Casa Migliaca.

The Queen's Biscuits

Biscotti regina

It is said that the people of Palermo believe this recipe produces the finest biscuits in the world—worthy of royalty, in fact, hence the name. We can only agree. This is Robert's interpretation of the biscuits we tasted at Casa Migliaca.

Makes approximately 40

olive oil
4 cups all-pupose flour
¾ cup sugar
½ teaspoon cinnamon
pinch of salt
½ cup butter, cut into small cubes
2 eggs, separated
¼ teaspoon vanilla extract
½ cup milk
1 cup sesame seeds

1. Preheat oven to 350°F and grease two cookie sheets.
2. Sift flour, sugar, cinnamon, and salt onto work surface. With your fingertips, toss butter through flour to create a coarse meal.
3. Make a well in the center and add egg yolks, vanilla extract, and most of the milk. Combine and knead to a firm dough. Add remaining milk if dough is too dry and crumbling. Cut into "fingers" measuring ½ x 1½ inches.
4. Lightly beat egg whites. Dip biscuits into egg white and roll in sesame seeds to coat.
5. Bake for 20–30 minutes until golden brown. Cool on wire racks. The biscuits will keep for 3 days stored in an airtight container.

Highlights of the Day

Gail

Kevin

Simon

Robert

Cows with Bells

Was this Sicily? It was more like an image from a Swiss chocolate wrapper. These cows wore bells! There they were, dotted among the olive trees, moving, and chewing to a chorus of musical notes. A swish of the tail, a shake of the head, and the sounds echoed through the mountains as if played through a quadraphonic stereo system.

The Queen's Biscuits

Maria Teresa made us a batch of the Queen's biscuits that afternoon. These are very traditional and produced in every town. They are rolled in sesame seeds, and we discovered that they are perfect to dip into the Malvasia delle Lipari of Carlo Hauner.

A Rustic Farmhouse

Casa Migliaca is what you might think of when you dream about an Italian country house—cool tiled floors, dark beams overhead, small windows with shutters, oddly shaped doors, stone sinks, a beautiful eighteenth-century kitchen, large oil-storage jars in the garden planted with geraniums and succulents, and massive, twisted old olive trees.

Fresh Almonds

Sebastiano told me that many people in Sicily eat green almonds, with their soft shells, or slice and cook them like porcini mushrooms. The trick is to pick them just before the kernel sets and the skin becomes leathery. At Casa Migliaca we had them with lovely soft cheese, a perfect combination.

143

From the Farm to the City

Friday, June 4

We are in no rush to leave Casa Migliaca for the big move to Palermo, where we will stay for three days. We meet and wander upstairs to the wondrous old kitchen for breakfast. Self-service is the goal here, and there's everything you could want. Robert takes on the role of cook, making delicious coffee, boiling the perfect three-minute egg, and slicing the various breads, cakes, and fruit.

This kitchen is inspiring, with its stone floors, beamed ceiling, and antique plates, platters, and utensils everywhere. I think we now have the basis of the renovations to our storage area at Donovans. I love this space and imagine how we might translate the atmosphere to St. Kilda.

Simon and I take one more stroll around the house to be sure we have documented all the different tiled, paved, and stone floors. Meanwhile, Kevin has a lengthy, luscious discussion with our host, Sebastiano, about the vines and wines of the area. Finally, we lazily pack up, pay the bill and say our farewells.

Back on the nightmare coast road we follow the map west along the northern edge of Sicily. Our first stop will be Cefalù, and from there we had planned to take the autostrada to Palermo. However, it appears the autostrada has yet to be finished because of a forty-year argument over who should pay for what. Construction has been under way for several years, but frequently stops for the argument to continue.

The sun is vicious from noon until 4:00 p.m., and it is boiling in Cefalù, a pretty coastal town that boasts a beautiful cathedral built in A.D. 1131. Much of the old town is intact and very quaint, with the twin towers of the cathedral looming above and surrounded by towering rocks. Kevin and I shelter under the shade of a bar umbrella while we watch the car, and Simon and Robert head off to check out the town and buy shoes. They both have very sore feet from the relentless walking we have done since our journey began.

Back on the autostrada at last, for the final push into Palermo. No one is particularly anxious about the drive into the city, but after reading all the guidebooks we are concerned about bad signals, traffic, and roads. We stop chatting as we get closer and closer to the city center, and from this point on we have our only dismal day so far. The high spirits we were in on the farm just a few hours ago disappear. The guidebooks were wrong. It is twice as bad as any of them say. Palermo seems to be the only city in the world where it is acceptable to drive completely on the wrong side of the road. Without Kevin's determination and delight at the challenge of driving into the city we would be giving up, hiring a cab, and following it to our hotel.

Happily, we arrive at last at the Grand Hotel Et Des Palmes, famous for being the place where the Mafia met in the 1950s and agreed to divide the Sicilian drug trade among themselves. The hotel rates four stars and is very expensive, but to us it looks as if it hasn't had a cent spent on it since that fateful meeting.

After a resolutely positive discussion about how lucky we are to have made it here in one piece and the wonderful history Palermo holds, we go out to discover the city's hidden treasures. It's hot, noisy, and quite unnerving. The streets are very dirty and everywhere we go, except the very expensive shops, people are rude to us. It is no use to have Robert translating; the locals appear even less inclined to help anyone who is not a native of Palermo. The gap between rich and poor here is magnified by the obvious wealth of some aspects of the city and the in-your-face poverty and neglect everywhere else. There is no middle ground at all. We visit a couple of museums, which seem to be in chaos. The city's treasures are well hidden.

We head back to the hotel at seven o'clock for a rest. At ten to nine the desk calls to say we cannot get the restaurant reservation we wanted, and our second choice turns out to be a disaster—even worse than not going out at all. Home early, we play cards but no one gets into it. We decide to start again tomorrow with a fresh outlook.

Gail

Avoid the Palermo Traffic

Never drive into Palermo! Better to stay at Mondello, a beachside area northwest of the city where you can leave your car at your hotel and catch a regular bus into Palermo. Mondello boasts plenty of restaurants and snack bars specializing in local seafood. We have all of this on good authority from a well-respected Palermitan.

Eating breakfast in the kitchen at Casa Migliaca

Highlights of the Day

Gail

Kevin

Simon

Robert

The Gallina

When I lived in Italy, my nickname was Gallina, a term of endearment meaning "hen" or "chicken." This nickname resurfaced during our trip, and the fluffy toy chicken we purchased at one of our garage stops became our mascot and good-luck charm. It served us well—and we sure needed it in Palermo.

The Drive into Palermo

Driving into Palermo took the competitive spirit of Italian driving to new heights, with all the drivers flexing their muscles for position. Without a detailed map, finding our hotel proved a grand challenge. My ego would not listen to Gail's suggestion of paying a taxi to lead us to our destination. Perhaps the two hours could have been shortened to 15 minutes?

A Difficult City

Somewhere just outside Palermo is an invisible border where the "romance" of Italy seems to run out. Palermo is a demanding city, fast, furious, and full of cars trying to get somewhere. The traffic defies description. Underneath all this, a beautiful city is hidden.

Colazione

The honest simplicity of breakfast (colazione) in Italy is captivating. The meal has remained pure amid ever-changing food trends and features the humblest of ingredients—toasted and buttered slices of newly baked bread, homemade jam, perfect ripe peaches, and freshly percolated coffee.

149

The Markets of Palermo

Saturday, June 5

The Palermo Tourist Congress is meeting in our hotel. I wonder what is on the agenda? A dose of city pride would be super. We are still feeling down because we expected more from this bustling, architecturally rich city. Everyone we have met in Italy to date has been kind and generous beyond our expectations, so what has happened to Palermo? There's a fascinating melting pot of people here who are all going so fast they don't see each other, let alone visitors.

We decide to cut our stay here short and depart tomorrow rather than Monday for Scopello. This will give us extra time to visit the much-anticipated ruins of Agrigento at the end of next week.

Our main reason for coming to Palermo was to visit the markets of Vucciria and Ballarò. The Vucciria is predominantly a fish market, especially in the piazza at its heart, while the Ballarò is more of a fruit and vegetable market. We recharge ourselves with a good breakfast and set off for the Vucciria. Walking down into it we realize how old it is. The buildings are in ruins—crumbling walls and timbers covered in weeds and overrun with stray cats. The market branches off in three or four directions down small streets. The sky is hardly visible, with a jigsaw puzzle of canvas protecting the stalls from the sun.

Initially it's fish, fish, fish—mountains of it. The tuna and swordfish are the size of whales and we stare in amazement. A man is boiling calamari to order in a big pot. You select your squirming little beast and within minutes it's boiled, sliced, squirted with lemon, and given a shake of cracked pepper, then served on a china plate while you stand, fork in hand, to eat it. The locals are shopping madly; after all, it is Saturday morning. The crowds around the fish stands jostle and shout for each piece of ruby-red tuna that is sliced. In fact things are so noisy, busy, and hands-on here that you need to wear a raincoat or some old clothes, as splattering is common.

Many of the fish of every color and shape we don't recognize, but they appear shining and fresh. Everywhere there are ribbons of pink, gold, silver, brown, and black perfectly piled goodies from the sea, with tails, fins, and eyes popping. Fresh herbs are also prominent, and their scent almost overwhelms the pungent odor of tons of seafood. Hot veal sliced into fresh bread, fish stew bubbling over a burner and stuffed into a crispy roll—there's no need to be hungry while you stroll around. We see baskets of tiny live snails crawling all over each other; the snails can be cooked to order in tomato sauce and parsley and served with a toothpick to dig them out of their shells.

The little streets leading from the fish stands also hold a feast for the eyes. Berry stalls, butchers, olive vendors, tomato-paste makers, goat carcasses with their coats still on, cheeses from all over Italy, tomatoes with big splashes of green and red, boxes of freshly baked onions, potatoes, peppers, and zucchini. I eat a most delicious lemon gelato scooped into a fresh brioche. It's only 9:30 a.m.—a little early in the day for us to eat any of the "real" food that surrounds us, but that's not stopping anyone else. We try a few snacks from a mobile vendor pushing his cart through the stalls and customers—chickpea fritters, rice balls with prosciutto, and cheese. It's the Vucciria's version of takeout, and takeout never smelled so good!

We continue to move along the winding narrow streets toward the Ballarò market; it takes about half an hour to get there. The housewares section is in what seems to be a long, thin passageway. You have to duck light fixtures and get used to tablecloths and lace curtains hanging across the street and hitting you in the face. Towels, tissues, toys, toiletries, electrical goods, CDs, plants, and clothes—I feel I need a big stick or machete to fight my way through. This is pickpocket heaven! Best not to carry a bag here, just a money belt.

Eventually the street opens up to the food area of the Ballarò—more fish, more fruit and vegetables, more food. We prefer this market to the Vucciria; it is bigger, cleaner, and cooler, and the atmosphere is much more local and friendly. The Vucciria is so involved in itself that there is hardly room for outsiders. In fact, all of us except Kevin found it quite creepy.

Nevertheless, we head back there to Trattoria Shanghai, which sits on a terrace overlooking the main square where the fish stalls are. From what we have read, Shanghai should be full of history. In fact, it is brutally run down, and we are scared to eat in case of food poisoning. We sit there worrying that the owner might decide at any moment to toss us over into the pit of swordfish below. And the hostess—she definitely has a degree from the Palermo Charm School.

We give up on Palermo and spend the afternoon in our room playing Sicilian cards. Dinner at a highly recommended restaurant is worse than the night before, and we can't wait to leave in the morning.

Late at night I try to reflect positively on the past two days. I remember a book I read recently that described Palermo as challenging. None of us has met the city head on and accepted the challenge. I think we have been completely spoiled by where we have been and the people we have met in the past two weeks. We had begun to feel like Italians without being Italian. All Palermo has really done is make us realize that we are visitors without the local knowledge to find the city's soul.

Gail

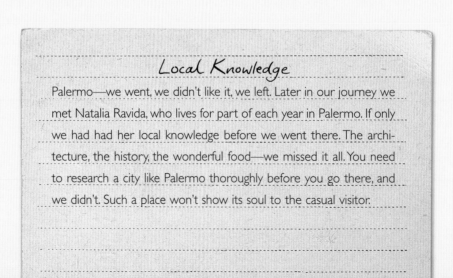

Local Knowledge

Palermo—we went, we didn't like it, we left. Later in our journey we met Natalia Ravida, who lives for part of each year in Palermo. If only we had had her local knowledge before we went there. The architecture, the history, the wonderful food—we missed it all. You need to research a city like Palermo thoroughly before you go there, and we didn't. Such a place won't show its soul to the casual visitor.

Rice Balls with Beef Ragù

Arancine

Literally translated as "little oranges," these rice balls are made in the same way as risotto and are probably the most popular way of eating rice in Sicily. Arancine appear all over Palermo but particularly in the markets, where food stalls serve them with a variety of fillings. They can be made over 2 days by preparing the filling on the first day and the rice on the second.

Makes 10–12

8 cups chicken stock
½ cup +2 tablespoons unsalted butter
2 pounds (about 5 cups) Arborio rice
8 saffron threads or ½ teaspoon powdered saffron
½ cup freshly grated Parmigiano-Reggiano
2 eggs, lightly beaten
2 cups breadcrumbs
olive oil

BEEF RAGÙ
1 pound ground lean beef
⅓ cup olive oil
½ onion, minced
1 stick celery, finely chopped
½ carrot, finely chopped
14 ounces canned, peeled Italian tomatoes with juice
chili flakes
salt
freshly ground black pepper

1. To make filling, brown meat over medium heat in a dry nonstick pan, stirring to break any lumps. Drain and discard any fat. In a saucepan, heat olive oil and fry onion, celery, and carrot until soft and barely golden. Add tomatoes, chili flakes, and meat. Cover and simmer for 30 minutes. Remove lid and simmer for an additional 15 minutes. Adjust seasoning and cool. Cover and refrigerate.

2. Place chicken stock in a saucepan and bring to a boil. Reduce to a simmer and maintain.

3. In a large saucepan, heat half the butter. Add rice and stir over medium–high heat for 2–3 minutes until grains are well coated and feel quite warm when touched with the back of the hand.

4. Add stock to rice approximately 1 cup at a time, stirring continuously until all liquid is absorbed before adding next quantity of stock. When you have used half the stock, stir saffron into rice. Continue adding stock until rice is al dente. Stir in cheese and remaining butter. Season and cool until just warm. Incorporate eggs into rice.

5. Wet your hands and gather up about ½ cup rice mixture. Form into a ball and flatten 1 side, making an indentation in the center. Place 1 heaped tablespoon of filling into hole, then seal well. Repeat this step until all rice has been used.

6. Coat each rice ball completely in breadcrumbs and chill for 15 minutes. Pan-fry in batches in olive oil until golden brown. Drain on paper towels and serve immediately.

Chickpea Fritters

Panelle

These "fast-food" items are sold by street vendors around Palermo's markets. They're fun to snack on while deciding which tomatoes to purchase.

Makes 12

olive oil
3 cups water
1½ cups chickpea flour
salt
freshly ground black pepper

1. Grease a cookie sheet. Combine water and flour in a saucepan, whisking to prevent lumps. Season with salt and pepper and cook in a saucepan over medium heat for 15–20 minutes until mixture begins to thicken. Stir continuously to stop mixture sticking to sides of pan.
2. Turn out batter onto baking tray and spread with a long, thin spatula to a thickness of ¼ inch. Cool.
3. Cut batter into squares, triangles, or circles. Pan-fry in olive oil until golden brown on both sides. Drain on paper towels, sprinkle with salt, and serve immediately.

Highlights of the Day

Gail

Kevin

Simon

Robert

Italian TV

There is nothing more corny than Italian television. Apart from the dubbed episodes of "Bonanza," "Flipper," and "I Dream of Jeannie," there are ads, mostly live and seemingly made up as they go. Even worse are the game shows, with women wearing next to nothing, flashing lights, and bad-taste hosts.

Overlooking the Market

A Chinese restaurant in the Vucciria in Palermo? No such luck. I came expecting to find the romance described by Peter Robb in his book "Midnight in Sicily." Alas, the romance had gone, but we had fun looking down at the goings-on in the market. A great place to capture the spirit of the Vucciria.

Those Vespas!

None of the congestion in the markets stopped the Vespas and motorbikes which continuously revved their engines, tooted their horns, and slowly pushed their way through as though the market was simply a nuisance.

Squid

Squid can be cooked in many ways. It is sometimes poached and then sliced and eaten in salads, especially when the squid is fresh and young and the salad oil is pristine. My favorite way is pan-fried with parsley and garlic stuffing and a good squeeze of lemon juice.

Sensational Scopello

Sunday, June 6

Most mornings, by the time we pack we are running late. Not today. By 7:00 a.m. we are waiting to have coffee and we've eaten, taken our luggage down to the lobby, and checked out by 8:05 a.m.

It turns out that the decision to leave Palermo early and on a Sunday is one of the best we've ever made. There is minimal traffic, and we arrive in Scopello by 9:15 a.m. Such a short trip in distance, but in charm, beauty, and hospitality it's another world. All of us feel relieved and happy to arrive. We drop our luggage at Pensione Tranchina and check out the small, busy town. Many people are arriving from Palermo, by car, and by boat, for a day at the beach.

The town is so small it only takes about 15 minutes to walk around. Perched on a ridge 200 yards above the sea, it is not much more than a piazza, a fountain, and three or four alleyways. There are two working pottery studios using original Scopello designs dating back to Moroccan times, two restaurants, a bakery, a grocery store, and two pensiones, and that's it!

Delicious caffè lattes are available at the bar in the tiny town square, along with fresh pastries and cookies baked by the signora in a small room behind the shop. She takes an instant shine to Kevin, wanting him to taste everything and insisting on having her photo taken with him. We are served a selection of little brioches filled with chocolate cream, custard, jam, preserved fruits, and tangy cheese. Just what we need, another breakfast—but who can resist!

The owners of Pensione Tranchina, Marisin and Salvatore, are accommodating and friendly, and give us suggestions for lunch and directions to the beaches. We quickly change into shorts and swimsuits and head back to the shops to buy food for a picnic. By now the tiny town is streaming with cars. It's hot, it's Sunday, the breeze is lovely, and Scopello couldn't be more beautiful.

Lunch is just as I love it—a super-long crunchy roll with the doughy center removed, rubbed on both sides with olive oil and filled with ripe tomatoes, cured sardines, and mozzarella cheese. It is baked in the oven to order and chopped into four. After choosing some luscious peaches and apricots from the grocery shop, we join the line of people at the town fountain, who are collecting water in every imaginable size and shape of container. The water is cold and slightly minerally, nothing like commercial bottled water. Then we pile into the car and go searching for a place to swim.

First stop is the site of the now-closed tuna factory. Only Italy could have a factory that looks like an old palace. High above it on a deserted peak is the tiny fortress that adorns every Scopello postcard. Three other towering rock formations, crowned with prickly pear, shoot up from the water.

The swimsuits here are so elegant I'm afraid to take off my T-shirt, which makes me look even more under-dressed. It's too hot to sit on the rocks, so we dive into the deep sea below. The water is so clear you can see legs and sand underwater for tens of feet.

The next beach on our list is in the Zingaro Nature Reserve, a fifteen-minute walk from where we park. The picnic is melting fast, and so are we.

If only we'd known. Everyone else has come here equipped with good walking or running shoes. We are wearing sandals. My platform designer footwear—the only chic thing I have for the beach—is especially inappropriate for the climb down the steep mountain track and I almost break my ankle twice.

The stunning little rock-covered beach is so crowded with people that it looks like a seal colony at the height of the mating season. All the flat ground is taken and we opt to perch on a cluster of bumpy rocks. We eat our now-soggy but still yummy rolls, and people-watch in between swims. Everyone has come with an umbrella and blow-up seats, pillows, thick blankets, or chairs to cushion them from the rocks. They have ice chests full of prosciutto, pasta, and fresh fruit, bottles of suntan oil, plastic shoes to wear in the water, and more. People are cramped so tightly

together it's hard to know who is with whom until the food starts to be served. How Italians can be so intolerant when driving and so easygoing in a crowded environment like this is beyond us.

Kevin, Simon, and I are the only white seals on the beach. At least Robert has some natural Italian color, but everyone else is golden brown or darker. We stagger across the pebbles to swim—without plastic shoes it's excruciating.

The sun is burning, so we walk back up the steep slope to the car and go home to shower and do our laundry. Washing our clothes has been a continuous problem. The system we've worked out is to put your foot over the plughole while you shower, then pour a generous amount of liquid soap in at your feet and stomp on the clothes. A nailbrush works for any tough stains. With garments hanging everywhere, our rooms soon look like a Chinese laundry, but the method works.

By late afternoon Scopello is bursting at the seams. We drink Campari and eat stunning blood orange juice sorbet in the signora's bar while watching the parade of cars and people pass within inches of our table. The crowds are varied—some people are very tall and dark with black almond-shaped eyes; others have light hair and vibrant green eyes. There are young and wealthy gold-clad trend-setters, moms and dads with lots of kids out for a picnic, old men playing cards, dogs sleeping under tables out of the sun, and motorbikes everywhere.

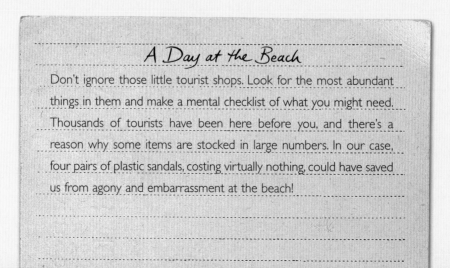

A Day at the Beach

Don't ignore those little tourist shops. Look for the most abundant things in them and make a mental checklist of what you might need. Thousands of tourists have been here before you, and there's a reason why some items are stocked in large numbers. In our case, four pairs of plastic sandals, costing virtually nothing, could have saved us from agony and embarrassment at the beach!

Dinner at Pensione Tranchina is served to the sixteen guests at individual tables, so there is no need to try to make conversation with strangers. I love this! Sometimes it's a relief after a long day. Marisin's food is from the heart. She serves a tasty pasta of linguine with peppers, and plates piled high with sweet red shrimp caught that afternoon, sprinkled with fresh breadcrumbs, lemon juice, and salt and pepper then oven-roasted. Even parts of the soft shells are worth eating. The beauty of these small fishing towns is that you have the chance to eat seafood that is only hours old.

Crusty bread, fresh fruit, and egg custard with rum-soaked amaretti biscuits follow, and the meal is topped off with almond biscuits and coffee. The local homemade wine is great and very alcoholic—Simon calls it "truth serum." As often happens after a very early start and a long adventurous day, over the wine we discover more about each other. Spending so many hours together—being continually challenged by moving, finding our way, and negotiating new things—brings us closer. We're just a little tired of packing and unpacking, but it's well worth it as the adventure continues.

We play cards until midnight and take a stroll outside for some fresh air. Surprise—no one has gone home and the town is buzzing. The gelateria and pizzeria have long lines, and the bar is crammed. The man selling wonderful little cones of roasted chickpeas, corn, chestnuts, and pistachios is surely never going to serve everyone in his line by sunrise.

At 4:00 a.m. we are awakened by the sirocco from Africa as it comes blowing fiercely through Scopello, whipping up the plastic cups and bits of paper left behind by the sunlovers. Salvatore knocks on our door to make sure we have secured our shutters against the wind. We drop back to sleep easily—a day at the beach, wonderful food, and safe, friendly surroundings have been just the tonic for a peaceful, well-earned rest.

Gail

Swimming near Scopello

The picturesque old tuna factory

Oven-roasted Shrimp with Breadcrumbs and Garlic

Gamberi rossi con aglio e mollica

A trip to the local fishing dock in Scopello yielded fabulous fresh shrimp for Marisin at Pensione Tranchina. She prepared them as all great cooks would—simply, letting their goodness jump from the plate. We reveled in the community of peeling and eating the shrimp and licking every morsel of the crumbs from our fingers.

Serves 4

¼ loaf casalinga bread
16–20 large shrimp
½–⅔ cup olive oil
1 teaspoon chili flakes
2 teaspoons freshly chopped Italian parsley
2 cloves garlic, finely chopped
salt
freshly ground pepper

1. Preheat oven to 350°F. In a food processor, process bread into coarse crumbs.
2. Put shrimp in a bowl and add breadcrumbs, olive oil, chili flakes, parsley, garlic, and a generous amount of salt and pepper. Toss to ensure shrimp are evenly coated.
3. Place shrimp in a single layer on a well-used baking tray. Bake until shells are rosy red, approximately 12 minutes.
4. Arrange shrimp on a large, decorative platter. Sit around the table and dig in.

Almond Curls

Biscotti ricci

These delicate cookies were served with coffee at the end of our meal at Pensione Tranchina.

Makes 24

4 cups blanched almonds *or* 2 cups almond meal
2 cups sugar
4 egg whites
½ teaspoon cinnamon
zest of 1 lemon

1. Preheat oven to 300°F. Grease and flour a cookie sheet.
2. If using whole almonds, grind to a fine meal in a coffee or spice grinder. Stir in sugar.
3. Beat egg whites until soft peaks form. Fold in almond mixture, cinnamon, and lemon zest. Mix well.
4. In a pastry bag fitted with a large notched nozzle, pipe S-shaped curlicues, approximately 3 inches long, onto the cookie sheet. Bake for 10–15 minutes until ridges on the cookies begin to brown.
5. Cool on a wire rack. Store in an airtight container.

Highlights of the Day

Gail

Kevin

Simon

Robert

The Fountain of Life
Scopello dates back to Norman times, and the town fountain seems as popular today as when it was the only source of water for the inhabitants. Lines of water-gatherers arrive nonstop as they have for hundreds of years. Water here is life itself!

The Mothers of Italy
I was captivated by the mothers in Italy. In a strange way they seemed to be drawn to me too. Perhaps it was the look of pleasure in my eyes at their attention to me. Perhaps I miss my childhood. Or maybe it's because I've lived away from my own mother for so long.

On the Beach
Would there be enough room for the four of us? Towels covered the whole beach, so close to each other that we were forced to step on many of them on our way to the water. But what beautiful people, with their designer swimsuits, gold jewelery, gourmet lunches, and tanned, happy faces.

Tinned Tuna
Tuna is a symbol of Sicily and the method of fishing is unchanged since medieval times. One catch can produce tons of tuna, so canning most probably came into existence as a way to cope with a sudden glut. I use canned tuna for pasta sauces and antipasti, but serve fresh tuna grilled, raw, or air-dried.

COMUNE DI RIPATRANSONE

TARIFFA DEL PANE E DELLA CARNE DAL *1° Giugno* AL *15 ?*

La Freri

No Man's Land

Monday, June 7

By early morning all is still after the wild winds of the night. The dust has settled and I can hear someone cleaning the street as we start another day in Sicily.

A relaxed breakfast at Pensione Tranchina is followed a little later by a caffè latte at the bar next door. The streets are almost completely empty—no noise, no cars, and the beachgoers who were running around everywhere like ants yesterday have disappeared. The only activity is tourists packing and leaving and elderly residents going about their business and stopping to chat to each other. Even the town dogs seem tired from the madness of yesterday.

We are not in a hurry to leave, given what is ahead—we are making for "the void," a part of Sicily that doesn't appear in any tourist book. It's a barren, thinly populated area that isn't used to tourists and has hardly any hotels to stay in. This southwestern tip of Sicily, just a short distance from Tunisia, may as well not exist, it seems. Our overnight stay will be in Mazara del Vallo, a big industrial fishing town not far from our eventual destination, Menfi, where tomorrow morning we have a special and much-anticipated meeting.

We take the autostrada to Mazara del Vallo and drop our luggage off at the very empty, unattractive hotel. This town is definitely not inviting, even a little scary. At the port on our way through the town we witnessed a fight with lots of blood.

We set off from the hotel back up to the town of Marsala for an appointment at Cantine Florio, the largest producer of Marsala wine in the world. It's only a thirty-minute drive, but the road is narrow and busy and full of frantic drivers intent on killing themselves and us. Marsala is a poor area suffering 30 percent unemployment. It is quite depressing—dry, barren, and lacking the life and vibrancy we have seen in other parts of Sicily. The green grapes growing for wine production are a relief compared to the rest of the landscape.

Sitting right on the sea and hidden away inside pristine gates is Cantine Florio. Its sheltered location gives relief from the sirocco winds, which are hotter and stronger here than they are in Scopello. We are welcomed with open arms by the director of Florio, Pietro Urso, a meeting facilitated by Antonio Carluccio, whom we met in Australia just three weeks ago. Signor Urso is delightful and invites us to join him for a memorable tasting and history lesson. Through successes, failures, and wars, Marsala wine has triumphed over all. In cooking, it is probably most widely known as the essential ingredient in great dishes such as veal scaloppine—and, of course, where would *zabaione* be without it? Pietro's assistant takes us on a fascinating tour where the history of the place unfolds before our eyes. We spend three wondrous hours surrounded by generous, knowledgeable people and the smell of liquid gold—well worth the trip.

We get a little lost driving back to Mazara del Vallo. I'm in the back and feel extremely nervous. The mixture of obvious poverty, a swirling hot wind, and total madness on the roads is getting to me. I'm truly relieved to get to the hotel, and Kevin is truly relieved to have me out of the car.

At the hotel desk we ask why the local police and *carabinieri* (who are even more important than the police) are patrolling the driveway and parking lot outside. The answer is that a judge lives nearby and they are protecting him from the Mafia. That's it for me. The receptionist asks Robert what I'm saying and he explains that I'm scared. She answers, "Don't worry, it's normal." Could this afternoon possibly get worse?

I'm convinced dinner won't be worth writing about and it isn't. Kevin misses out on the grand couscous experience he was so looking forward to. Our research had told us that couscous is common in this area, but it seems this is only in private homes, not restaurants.

After the meal we are too scared to go outside and explore, despite Kevin's protests. We drink a soothing limoncello in the hotel bar while Simon and Robert voice their displeasure at having rooms on the same side of the building as the judge's apartment. We try to calm them, saying nothing will happen, but deep down I'm extremely relieved that Kevin and I have a room on the opposite side of the hotel. We sleep, but not well.

Gail

Alternative Routes

If you plan to take a similar trip to ours, try an alternative route via Erice, a beautiful medieval town just a short drive from Palermo. Trápani, a big fishing town, is another option. From there, an early start will allow a visit to Marsala and Cantine Florio, and then a long drive through "no man's land" to the bustling fishing town of Sciacca.

Sautéd Veal with Marsala Sauce

Scaloppine di vitello alla Marsala

Our visit to Cantine Florio brought back to our hearts this most traditional dish. Simple in its preparation and execution, it requires, as do all dishes, the best-available ingredients. Perfect accompaniments are Roasted Peppers Under Oil (see page 62) and simple boiled potatoes.

Serves 4

salt
freshly ground black pepper
flour
17 ounces prime-quality veal, cut into ¼-inch slices
3 tablespoons unsalted butter
¼ cup olive oil
1 cup best-quality Marsala

1. Season the flour and dip the veal slices in it. Pat each slice firmly with the palms of your hands in order to remove excess flour and ensure an even dusting.
2. Heat butter and olive oil in a skillet or frying pan over medium-high heat and fry the veal slices on both sides until nicely browned. Do not crowd slices in the pan—this will result in steamed meat rather than high-heat frying. If butter and oil become too brown or burn, discard and add a fresh quantity. Cover veal slices and keep warm.
3. Add Marsala to pan and deglaze, reducing liquid by two-thirds. Return all meat to pan and simmer for 1–2 minutes until sauce begins to thicken. Season with salt and pepper.
4. Serve meat on warm plates with a few spoonfuls of sauce over the top.

Zabaglione

Zabaione

This is one of the most famous culinary uses for Marsala. Zabaglione can be served warm or cold, and is a perfect accompaniment to the season's freshest fruit or a chocolate biscotti. It is also an essential ingredient in the famous Italian dessert tiramisu.

Makes 1 cup

water
3 large egg yolks
3 tablespoons sugar
½ cup best-quality dry Marsala

1. Half-fill a medium-sized saucepan with water and bring to a boil. In a stainless steel or glass bowl of a size that will sit on top of the saucepan, combine egg yolks and sugar and whisk until yolk thickens slightly and turns lighter in color. Add Marsala slowly and mix thoroughly.
2. Set bowl on top of saucepan of boiling water and stir continuously for 10–15 minutes until mixture is thick enough to coat the back of a spoon. Do not boil.
3. Remove bowl from saucepan and continue to stir for a few minutes to assist in cooling. Transfer zabaglione to a clean bowl and cool completely. Refrigerate and use within 4 hours.

Highlights of the Day

Gail   Kevin   Simon   Robert

The Bombola

There is no natural gas in Sicily; it is all bottled. When I lived in Sicily long ago the "bombola man" would rattle up and down the streets in his "ape" (tiny truck) with ten or twelve gas bottles in the back, calling, "Bombola, bombola." Today it is exactly the same, with the gas man still heard in almost every town in Sicily.

Dreaming of Couscous

Sicilian cooking is incredibly regional. Trying to find couscous on the east coast of the island was impossible. "Go to the west," I was told. But the hotel receptionist in Mazara del Vallo told me I would never find it in a restaurant even there. Didn't I know that it takes five hours to prepare? My dream of tasting the Sicilian version of this Arab import was still unfulfilled.

Sirocco

BANG, BANG, BANG! Was I awake or asleep? A voice screamed, in Italian I think, to close the shutters. They were banging all over town as the sirocco arrived, dust, papers, and leaves caught in its breath. I lay in bed listening to the strange whistling, swirling howl engulfing the village. By morning all was calm again.

Zabaglione with Marsala

Zabaglione is a delicious whipped foam of Marsala wine, egg yolks, and sugar. My mother used to make it for breakfast. Some say that it comes from the French "sabayon," but I believe it has Arabic roots. "Zabbina," a Sicilian word which comes from the Arabic, means "to whip while cooking."

Wines of Cantine Florio

"Marsala is a drink of meditation and thinking." So began Pietro Urso, the director of Cantine Florio, when he received us at his impressive facility in the historic port town of Marsala.

It all began in 1773 when John Woodhouse, a Liverpool merchant, loaded his ship with a quantity of barrels of Sicilian wine. In order to stabilize the wine for the long voyage back to England, Woodhouse added alcohol spirit. The wine acquired an interesting richness and gained immediate success as an alternative to port, sherry, and Madeira; its popularity led Woodhouse to set up his own production business in the town of Marsala. The wine gained a wider reputation when another Englishman, Benjamin Ingham, set up a second establishment and was able to increase distribution to markets beyond Europe, notably America and Australia.

In 1833, Vincenzo Florio established yet another production house, further refining winemaking techniques and, more importantly, distribution. After years of success, Cantine Florio acquired the Woodhouse and Ingham firms in 1929, making it the largest force in Marsala wine production.

The town is blessed with a perfect location on the west coast of Sicily, in the heart of the Mediterranean sun-belt. The special microclimate with its limited temperature changes within the seasons, the mineral-rich soils that are dry and warm, and the exposure to African winds carrying sea brine to the grapes, all join to make Marsala wine unique.

To the uninitiated, Marsala is a sweet, rich dessert wine. However, our exposure to the range at Cantine Florio revealed a great variety of interesting offerings including:

- Vintage Vecchioflorio—an excellent dessert wine that is deep amber with gold reflections and has hints of raisins, bitter almonds, and vanilla. Aged for at least three years, it contains a white-wine base with the addition of wine brandy and cooled wine, which adds its "paint of amber." It is served chilled and, though sweet, makes an excellent aperitif or after-dinner wine with a light dessert.
- Vintage Vecchioflorio Riserva—contains all the elements of the Vecchioflorio with a finer degree of intensity. It is served cool and is best with dried fruit or a rich dessert. It is aged for at least six years.
- Vintage Vecchioflorio Vergine—made from a white-wine base and wine spirit, this Marsala is produced only in the best vintages. It is characterized by an intense bouquet and a full, soft, dry flavor. Served cool, this is an elegant aperitif. It is aged for at least seven years.

- Vintage Vino Marsala Vergine "Terre Arse"—this superb aperitif style is delicate, with flavors of bitter almonds and burnt honey, and is aged for at least nine years. It is served chilled with canapés.
- Vintage Baglio Florio—at the top of the range, this delicate Marsala is made only in outstanding vintages. Served chilled, it is dry, warm, and lively with suggestions of licorice and almonds. Because of its special quality, it is aged for at least twelve years.

Our tour included a tasting of all these fine wines under the expert tutelage of Signor Urso, plus a visit to the cellars. Actually above ground, the massive aging facility contains a highway of barrels and covers an area of 25,000 square meters. The aging process is critical to the finished product, starting in 475-gallon Slovenian red oak casks and finishing in 80-gallon French oak casks. The facility is quiet, almost tranquil—a necessary factor in the aging of this fine wine. The clay walls are covered with tiles and the high, vaulted ceiling ensures proper internal aeration and a steady year-round temperature. These are ideal conditions for the long, slow maturation of Marsala wines.

A visit to Cantine Florio is not complete without viewing the museum, where wines dating back to 1929 rest gracefully on the shelves. We compared our visit to a religious experience, with none of us daring to speak for fear of disturbing the repose of the priceless crusted bottles. Signor Urso explained that there would have been many more had Cantine Florio not been destroyed during the Allied invasion of Sicily on the way to freeing Europe in World War II. He said that so much wine was destroyed during that fateful time that the Mediterranean Sea smelled of Marsala for a week.

Kevin

Olive branch
from Ravida

Villa Ravida

Tuesday, June 8

Early, early, early we're up and away, heading west along the southern coast of Sicily for Menfi, an eighteenth-century town which was devastated in 1968 by an earthquake and has never recovered. More than 60 percent of its buildings collapsed, while some of the surrounding towns were completely destroyed.

Anyone without a substantial reason to visit Menfi would probably stay on the autostrada and zoom right past. But we have an appointment with Signor Nicola Ravida at his villa. Ravida olive oil was the first Sicilian oil to win in competition, in 1993. It has continued to win gold medals in various competitions and now sells worldwide. Prior to Ravida, competition judges and world oil connoisseurs would never have considered a Sicilian oil even worthy of tasting. The now-converted experts describe its taste as that of freshly mown grass, intensely herbal, and with a hint of the sea. I just think it's delicious.

I discovered the wonderful oils made by Ravida on the shelves of Philippa's Bakery and the Richmond Hill Cafe and Larder in Melbourne. Somehow I missed the story about Villa Ravida published in a local food magazine, but managed to make contact through the Internet. The villa was built in the 1700s as the family's summer residence and is considered one of the finest examples of Sicilian neoclassical architecture in existence. I knew when I saw photographs and drawings of the villa in a gourmet tour brochure that I had to go there.

We had several phone conversations with Nicola and exchanged quite a few faxes before our trip. Because the villa was going to be fully booked at the time of our visit we were unable to stay there, but luckily, today the resident group will be away at the markets in Palermo. In their absence, Nicola has kindly invited us on a tour of "La Gurra," the family's farm property, followed by lunch back at Villa Ravida.

By 9:30 a.m. we are outside the given address, parked near a high wall surrounded by concrete apartment blocks. We assume that this is their town house and that the villa itself is on the farm. How wrong we are. Behind the gates is Villa Ravida itself—my dream house. We are greeted by Nicola, his daughter Natalia, who handles the marketing arm of Ravida, and his wife Signora Ninni, who leaves quickly to prepare for our lunch. Nicola speaks excellent English. He divides his time between Menfi and Rome, where he works as a consultant. Natalia was until recently a leading journalist in London but now moves between Palermo, where she met her husband, and Menfi, her birthplace.

They are a wonderful working family—Nicola with his

love and knowledge of La Gurra and its splendid olives, and Natalia with her love of Ravida and her worldly business sense. She is responsible for finally convincing Nicola, in 1991, to start bottling the oil for sale. It took her four years before that to persuade him that the oil was worthy of being used for more than just the family's personal home cooking or being sold in bulk at the local cooperative.

The villa's exterior is breathtaking. Our favorite kind of paving—river pebbles meticulously laid in mosaic patterns—leads to wide stone steps and a large landing with four huge sandstone pillars, capped by an even more beautiful Doric sandstone tiara. The building resembles a monument or temple to the Greek gods. Inside, it has been allowed to age gracefully, with worn, wobbly, original Sicilian tiles beautifully set into the floor, damask-covered fringed furniture, a delicious combination of antiques and personal mementos, flaking ceiling frescoes, and a wonderful sense of style in every room.

The ceiling frescoes, in vibrant reds, greens, and yellows, show a history of decorating styles and changing tastes. Each generation at the villa has contributed its own design, varying from Second Empire flowers to medallions. In one room, directly below some Empire flowers is a neoclassical frieze, almost military in style. In another room the ceiling looks Egyptian, while the room has tiny gilt chairs, muted gold and brocade silk loungers, dark chestnut tables, and sheer linen drapes in various colors adorning tall, glass-paned French doors. These open onto several terraces and a view of the vegetable gardens below.

The central sitting room drops down to a formal dining room edged with comfortable furniture. Dark, religious-themed oil paintings cover the white-washed walls almost from floor to ceiling. The table is set ready for lunch in olive-green damask. The house drops down again to a stunning kitchen, full of old copper pots, and an adjoining courtyard garden set for the resident guests on their return from Palermo. A dream!

In the cellars we learn about the various oils and how they are judged, why Ravida oil is so good, where it is sold, when it became recognized as a top product, and especially how passionate both of these gorgeous people are about what they do and the first-class oil they produce. Already under its spell before we came to Villa Ravida, for us the oil is beyond compare.

Our tour of the farm, 3 miles north of the villa, emphasized the dedication and work involved in making the oil. La Gurra is in perfect olive-farming country—it has clean air and is completely organic and free of any pesticides or non-natural products. The 300-year-old olive trees are the heart of the Ravida groves. Many have been left to grow wild, thus allowing visitors to see what the landscape would have been like before farming began. At harvest time the farmhouse used to be home to the Ravida family and forty-odd pickers. La Gurra also produces excellent cabernet sauvignon and merlot grapes.

Oils Ain't Oils

Do yourself a favor and purchase a bottle of exquisite extra-virgin olive oil. Get some crusty bread, set out three or four dishes of varying oils—including your new purchase—and have your own blind tasting. You'll soon realize that tasting beautiful oils is no different from tasting fine wines.

Back at the villa Ninni appears, immaculately dressed, and shows us to the dining room. Everything is home-produced and appears on the table as we have come to expect from these family experiences. Served by a house-maid in a black and white uniform, there are scrumptious little pieces of dried bread with a paste of olives, capers, and mint, accompanied by excellent Sicilian wine. We have a sweet and salty tomato tart, fried sardines and calamari, fresh steamed shrimp, involtini of eggplant straight from the oven, a delicious bean salad, fresh fruit, and dynamic coffee-and-chocolate semifreddo.

Silver pots of coffee are served later on the terrace while we chat about food, the local wines and culture, the beautiful olives, and of course the much-loved oil. We also talk about the Mafia, which has been on our mind the last few days, especially since Mazara del Vallo. Comments are made regarding how completely disgruntled the people of Sicily are with politics and the Mafia. However, the events of recent years have at least convinced them that the Mafia's power has declined and that it is no longer invincible.

Our departure is much later than expected. They ask us to stay for dinner—such generosity—but we must leave for Agrigento. The ruins await. After about an hour's drive, we arrive at the Villa Athena, definitely the only place to stay in this town. It is within walking distance of the ruins and situated so that you don't have to see the actual town, whose beautiful beaches and hills have been spoiled by overdevelopment and petrochemical plants—a shame.

We check in and settle by the pool, which is a welcome relief from the heat. After a swim and a shower we meet in the garden for a cool drink and to look at the spectacular view, one to remember for the rest of our lives. There it stands, perched on the hill, 2600 years old—the floodlit Temple of Concord, golden against a black sky and showing off its towering sandstone columns.

Dinner is fresh fish from the outdoor grill with a crisp salad, and off we go to sleep. Tomorrow we enter the Valley of the Temples.

Gail

Entrance to Villa Ravida

Old frescoes on the walls

Villa Ravida has been allowed a wonderful sense of style

to age gracefully, and has
n every room.

181

Summer Salad of Beans and Tomato

Insalata di fagioli e pomodoro

This simple but delightful salad was served with our lunch at Villa Ravida. Its flavor was heightened by the freshest young green beans and the ripest cherry tomatoes.

Serves 4

1 pound young green beans, trimmed
2 baskets very ripe cherry tomatoes, halved (about 1 pound)
Ravida olive oil
white vinegar
sea salt
freshly ground black pepper

1. Steam beans until tender and refresh under cold water.
2. In a bowl, combine beans and tomatoes. Add olive oil and a few drops of white vinegar to coat. Season and toss. Chill thoroughly.
3. Just before serving add a little more olive oil and vinegar, if desired. Adjust seasoning and serve.

Villa Ravida's Green Olive Spread

Olivada verde alla Villa Ravida

Following our olive-oil tasting in the cellars of Villa Ravida, we enjoyed this brightly flavored spread on toasted bread with glasses of crisp white wine. The spread is at its best when it is absolutely fresh.

Makes about 2 cups

⅓ cup Ravida olive oil
6 anchovies
2 tablespoons capers
5–6 mint leaves
1 cup green olives, pitted
salt
freshly ground black pepper

1. Combine olive oil, anchovies, capers, and mint in a food processor and blend until smooth.
2. Add olives and pulse in bursts. The mixture needs to be moist and spreadable but still have texture.
3. Season with salt and a liberal amount of freshly ground pepper. Serve immediately on toasted bread.

Coffee Chocolate Semifreddo

Semifreddo di caffè e cioccolato

Literally translated, semifreddo means chilled. It is an excellent creamy dessert which doesn't require an ice-cream machine. Do not spare any expense—use the best-available chocolate. Amarena cherries, with their rich, concentrated syrup, are a superb accompaniment. They are available at Italian food stores.

Serves 6

9 ounces best-quality dark chocolate
¼ cup very strong espresso coffee
6 eggs, separated
⅓ cup Cognac *or* fine brandy
1¼ cups cream

1. Line a 1-quart terrine mold with plastic wrap.
2. Set a stainless steel bowl over a saucepan of boiling water. Place chocolate and espresso in bowl and melt chocolate. Remove from heat and whisk in egg yolks one at a time. Stir in Cognac.
3. Whip cream until it forms soft peaks (do not overwhip). Fold cream into chocolate mixture.
4. In a clean bowl, whip egg whites until they form soft peaks (do not overwhip). Fold into chocolate cream. Pour mixture into mold and freeze for 3–4 hours.
5. Unmold and serve with sliced fresh cherries or Amarena cherries in their syrup.

184

Highlights of the Day

Gail · Kevin · Simon · Robert

A Romantic Man
On the terrace of Villa Ravida, drinking coffee and eating cherries, we talked with Nicola and Ninni for hours. Nicola loves the full moon with a passion, loves his olive trees, and loves touching the lives of the people who visit the villa. "A true romantic," Kevin said as we drove away. I agree!

Limoncello
In Sicily I came to relish the digestif limoncello, taken at the end of a meal. It is made by steeping lemon peel in alcohol for fifteen days and then blending with sugar syrup. My head rested peacefully on the pillow with the scent of lemons in my nostrils and a vision in my mind of citrus orchards glistening in the sun.

Gentle Decay
"In a state of gentle decay" is how I would describe Villa Ravida, a house that is formal, almost grand, as well as a family home that is lived in and greatly loved. I feel lucky to have seen her faded, frescoed ceilings, lustrous tiled floors, grand old pieces of furniture waxed and polished year after year, silk upholstery, and dark oil paintings.

Sicilian Olives
Olives were cultivated in Iran about 5000 years ago and then spread to Italy, and of course Sicily, which has the ideal climate for them. There are dark luminous black olives, giant green olives, little coal-black olives, smoky berry-like olives from Menfi, and olives of all the greens of the Sicilian sea at dusk.

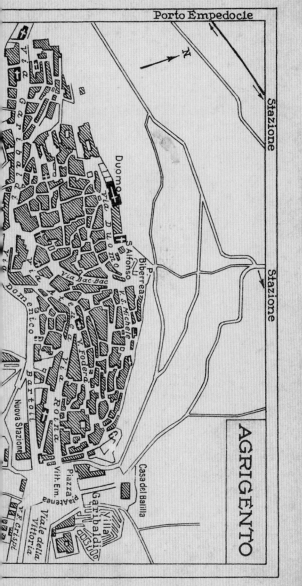

Porto Empedocle

AGRIGENTO

in Italy by the E.N.I.T. (Italian State Tourist Department)

IND. GRAF. BESOZZI - MILANO

AGRIGENTO

ENTE NAZIONALE INDUSTRIE TURISTICHE
FERROVIE DELLO STATO

The Ruins

Wednesday, June 9

The phone rings early. It's our travel agent and good friend, Judy Gillard. She's working in a town in Lake Como, in Italy's north, and is calling to see how our trip has gone so far. It's so great to speak to a friend from home and I instantly feel a little sad thinking about Melbourne.

Judy tells us all the world news and that everyone is fine at home and at Donovans. She's just checking to see if we need her to make some calls to our airline to deal with excess baggage. We sure do—good thinking on her part. Maybe we won't need to mortgage the house to pay for all that luggage after all.

Our room smells bad. Kevin checks out the air-conditioner and it's full of moldy water. We switch it off, convinced we have solved the problem.

Off we go—four serious explorers! Just a short walk down the road, up some steps and there they are—the ruins. Big, overpowering ruins. Agrigento, called Akragas by the Greeks, was a very prosperous community in Magna Graecia. Everyone wanted to live here, from the Greeks to the Carthaginians with their wealth, building skills, and aqueducts. The court of Terone brought poetry and musicians while the period of Empedocle brought democratic government. The Carthaginians fortified the city from threat

and later used it as their military base to fight off the Romans. The Romans eventually captured the city, and it flourished and spread. And so the history continued—Saracens, Normans, Romans again. Eventually this ancient city was robbed of its wealth and treasures, never to recover.

Today Agrigento is a magical place of ruins that must be seen. I sit quietly for a moment and the past engulfs me, sending my imagination into a spin. Amid the yellow and gold-colored stone of monumental proportions, I can hear the shuffle of sandal-clad feet and robes dragging in the dust, and feel the buzz of the community that once lived here.

Halfway through the exploring I opt to stay with the camera gear and bottles of water while Simon, Kevin, and Robert head for Tempio di Giunone, the Temple of Juno. The shady olive tree I'm resting beneath undergoes its own invasion soon after the crew heads up the hill, as buses of tourists start to arrive. My blissful daydream of chariots and worshippers at the temple ends. The tour groups are dropped at one end of the long road and proceed down to where they are collected at the base of the hill. My tree, halfway along the road, happens to be the only shade, so each tour guide halts his group there for an explanation speech and relief from the sun.

There is one invasion after another, and I have too much gear to move. I'm sitting absolutely in the middle, like an alien. First come the Americans—that's fine, the love of my life is an American. I stay silent, but it's to no avail as they insist on knowing who I am and what I'm doing. The next wave is Dutch; they don't ask me a thing, just take me as part of the olive tree. Next come the Italians—they all light cigarettes at once and it's a wonder the parched olive tree doesn't go up in flames. The invasions continue every ten minutes for the next hour and I want to laugh out loud as I realize this would make a great Fellini movie. I also become the on-site photographer as more and more people hand over their cameras for me to take happy snaps. At last, to my relief, the temple explorers return and we head away from the serious swarms of tourists, back to the hotel and out of the heat.

Our room smells much worse; in fact it now can't be tolerated and we have to move. No one can explain it. The hotel clerk simply hands over the key to the room next door, tells us to move our things and says they will clean the room later. In our new room the shower is dripping and the TV is on. I wonder if they haven't made a mistake and the previous occupant has just gone out for a moment. We never find out what the smell is, but another unsuspecting guest sleeps with it that night.

The pool is a wonderful relief from the heat. We have a swim, a sandwich, and some fruit and rest a little after experiencing the ruins—a piece of history almost too enormous to fathom. Everyone is tired and we lie by the pool for hours, watching all the other guests, young and old, baking their bodies in full sun and continually spraying themselves with oil. No anti-skincancer campaign here! We four explorers huddle under the only umbrella, covered in sunscreen.

Simon, Robert, and I aren't motivated to go out to dinner, but Kevin, always determined, convinces us that dining in the hotel restaurant for a second night would waste the chance for local exploration. I guess we don't really want to suffer another night listening to the pianist and synthesized drum machine playing Frank Sinatra songs, being served by waiters dressed like the captain on *The Love Boat*, gold braid and all. Kevin has read about a particular restaurant and asks the reception clerk to book us a table.

At 8:30 p.m. we're in a cab, feeling much better from the relaxation by the pool. We've dressed up a little and everyone is in good spirits. The ten-minute ride to the restaurant is amazing as we discover more ruins, all lit and glowing, around every corner. Alas, the hotel clerk forgot to tell us our reservation was not made. In fact, the restaurant is closed.

As has happened so often on this trip, good things come from bad situations. Luckily we have the nicest taxi driver in Italy. He assures us he will take us somewhere he likes to eat, which although a little out of the way has good food and good service. It's called Le Caprice. Prior to attacking the self-serve antipasto we select our own fresh

Soldier On

Traveling, while it is often wondrous, can also be very disappointing. Whenever we arrived somewhere that was not up to our expectations, our natural instinct was to sulk. However, Kevin always encouraged us to get into the car or take a walk and look for another highlight we would otherwise have missed. It's a great attitude to have. Bravo Kevin!

fish for main course from the display. Sole is the ticket for the boys and I choose a fish there is no name for, but which I'm assured is the best there and rarely available.

The antipasto is the most sparkling, alive food we have seen for days. Strange how sometimes you know even before you have the first mouthful that it's good cooking and will taste wonderful. There's frittata made with local cheese, deep-fried sardines, involtini, marinated swordfish, oven-roasted onions, slightly pickled vegetables, fresh baby asparagus, green beans, eggplant three ways, fresh artichokes, tiny snails in tomato sauce, and big olives, crushed olives, chili olives, and tiny olives, all cured on the premises.

The fish is simply grilled, beautifully seasoned with lemon, and comes with a fresh green salad to dress yourself with the first-quality oil and vinegar on the table. The waiter brings a plate of house-cut deep-fried french fries as a gesture for Kevin—he recognizes his accent. We love it all, including the delicious local wines. My no-name fish turns out to be a sensation, a little like the Murray cod I've had at the Flower Drum restaurant at home in Melbourne. Semifreddo, crème caramel, and ricotta cake follow.

What a meal, and so unexpected. Kevin was right to venture out. One thing about Kevin—he never gives up. It's what you need on a trip like this because you never know when you will stumble onto something so good it's unforgettable.

The taxi driver is waiting to take us home. At the hotel the four of us sit silently in the dark with glasses of Sicily's sumptuous limoncello, staring at the great floodlit ruins of Agrigento and thinking of all the people who have sat in the cool of the evening like this over the past two and a half thousand years.

Gail

Temple of Concord

Asparagus Frittata

Frittata con asparagi

This was one of our favorites among the many delectable creations in the antipasto selection at Le Caprice.

Serves 6

1 pound asparagus
6 large eggs
¼ cup freshly grated Parmigiano-Reggiano
salt
freshly ground black pepper
3 tablespoons unsalted butter
freshly snipped tarragon, parsley, *or* chives

1. Trim asparagus and remove tough outer skin with a vegetable peeler. Steam until tender and refresh under cold water.
2. Preheat oven broiler. In a bowl, lightly beat eggs with cheese. Season and add asparagus, stirring to combine.
3. Melt butter in a 8-inch frying pan. Pour in egg and asparagus mixture, arranging asparagus in rows. Reduce heat to low and cook until eggs are just set and top is still uncooked.
4. Place pan under broiler and cook until top is set and frittata is golden brown. Slide out of pan with a spatula and scatter with fresh herbs. Serve immediately.

Stuffed Sardines

Sarde ripieni

This recipe uses the traditional stuffing from *Sarde a beccafico, a classic Sicilian dish.* The sardines are rolled into small involtini after stuffing and then baked tails up. The name was given to the dish because when arranged in the pan the sardines look like little beccafichi—warbler birds—pecking at the pan.

Serves 4

2 pounds (approximately 20) fresh sardines, cleaned and gutted
4 medium-sized onions, cut into ¼-inch slices
20 thin slices lemon
20 fresh bay leaves
¼ cup olive oil
lemon wedges

STUFFING
⅓ cup sultanas
¼ cup olive oil
1 medium-sized onion, finely chopped
1 cup breadcrumbs
⅓ cup pine nuts
⅓ cup orange juice
⅓ cup lemon juice
salt
freshly ground black pepper
pinch of sugar

1. To make stuffing, soak sultanas in lukewarm water for 10 minutes. Preheat oven to 375°F. Heat olive oil in a skillet or frying pan and fry onion until light golden. Add breadcrumbs and stir constantly over medium–high heat until crumbs are lightly toasted. Remove from heat.
2. Drain sultanas and add to breadcrumb mixture with pine nuts and orange and lemon juice. Season with salt and pepper. Taste, and if mixture is too tart add sugar.
3. Fill each sardine with 1 tablespoon of stuffing, 1 onion slice, and 1 lemon slice. Arrange in a baking dish and attach 1 bay leaf to each sardine with a toothpick. Drizzle olive oil over.
4. Bake for 20–30 minutes. Serve warm or at room temperature with lemon wedges.

Ricotta Cake

Torta di ricotta

This delicate cake is lighter than a traditional cheesecake. Ricotta is a by-product of cheese-making and is better described as a milk product than a cheese. Meaning "re-cooked," it is made from the whey after it has been separated from the curd. The whey is gently heated until the ricotta forms on the surface.

½ cup sultanas
¼ cup Marsala
2 pounds ricotta
6 eggs
¼ cup all-purpose flour
⅔ cup sugar
1 teaspoon cinnamon
1 teaspoon nutmeg
1 tablespoon vanilla extract
zest of 1 lemon
zest of 1 orange
¼ cup apricot jam

1. Preheat oven to 325°F. Butter and flour a 10-inch springform pan. Soak sultanas in Marsala for at least 1 hour.
2. Fit electric mixer with paddle attachment and beat ricotta at low speed until it is homogenous. While ricotta is mixing, lightly whisk eggs. Add approximately 1 egg at a time to ricotta until incorporated, then add flour, sugar, and sultanas, blending completely. Add cinnamon, nutmeg, vanilla, lemon, and orange zest. Blend completely.
3. Pour into springform pan and bake for 1–1½ hours until filling is set. Test that cake is done by pressing lightly in the center with your fingertips. If cake springs back, cooking is complete. Turn off oven and let cake cool in oven with door open.
4. Warm apricot jam over low heat. Release sides of springform pan and brush top of cooled cake with jam. This cake may be refrigerated for up to 2 days, but be sure to allow it to come to room temperature before serving.

Amid the yellow and gold-colored stone of monumental proportions,

I can hear the shuffle of sandal-clad feet and robes dragging in

the dust and feel the buzz of the community that once lived here.

Highlights of the Day

Gail · **Kevin** · **Simon** · **Robert**

Here's to Sardines

In Sicily, sardines are special and treated with the respect they deserve. They can be simply prepared under good oil with a big squeeze of lemon, or filled with breadcrumbs, seasoned, and rolled involtini-style and baked, or oven-roasted under mountains of sweet onions, or quickly floured and fried and served crunchy, tails and all.

Pure Espresso

The best espresso is a gulp or two of intensely concentrated liquid. I thought such a potent drink would result in bitterness. On the contrary — as the water content is so low, the brief pressure extracts only the purest essence, and the resulting caffeinated gem is remarkably smooth-sipping.

The Magic of Ruins

Strange, isn't it, how ruins can stir the mind and soul? Imagine all the eyes that have marveled at the sheer beauty of these stones at Agrigento, and all the famous feet that have clambered in or around the ruins, from Greek philosophers to people of all the nations that have conquered and lost Sicily.

Fragrant Wine of the Romans

In the fourth century A.D., when the Romans were in Agrigento, they made a scented wine by first placing some green citron leaves in a small basket made of palm branches. This was put into a wide-mouthed jar of fresh wine, to ferment. After forty days, the leaf basket was lifted out and the wine stored in an earthenware pot. It was mixed with a little honey to drink.

195

The Monastery in the Mountains

Thursday, June 10

We leave Sicily tomorrow, but there's one more adventure ahead of us. From Agrigento we plan to travel north back into the Madonie mountains to the very heart of Sicily. We are to stay at a fourteenth-century monastery just past Gangi, halfway between Palermo and Taormina, called Tenuta Gangivecchio.

As usual, we get lost on the way. No one is amused, especially Kevin. The roads are narrow, constantly under repair, and very busy, and we are silent and on the edge of our seats until we hit the autostrada, which relieves the tension for an hour or so.

About an hour out of Agrigento we stop at a town called Caltanissetta to purchase another travel bag for the multitude of things we have collected. This is the last big town before we leave the autostrada for the mountains. The guidebooks told us that it was in the middle of nowhere, but they are completely wrong. It's a wonderful oasis of a town, obviously in a wealthy and prosperous area. It boasts a large university, wonderful winding streets of exquisite stores, friendly helpful people, and a sensational market which is crowded with people and packed with luscious produce.

We would love to spend more time in Caltanissetta, but there's a challenge ahead and we need to keep going

if we are to reach Gangivecchio for lunch. The scenery changes dramatically as we get farther away from the coast, the olive groves and grapevines slowly disappearing to be replaced by fields of wheat. Given the amount of bread consumed in Italy, it is no surprise that life is prosperous here. Once off the autostrada, the 25 miles or so to Gangivecchio take two hours.

The monastery sits off to the side of the road on a sloping hill. The old building, in which our hosts the Tornabene family live, has some 120 rooms—plenty of space for one family! Mother Wanda and daughter Giovanna are in charge of the kitchen. Their cooking is famous throughout Sicily and on weekends people flock from all directions, traveling long distances to eat the enthusiastic, authentic food. The recipes are distinctive and come from the family tradition, and we can't wait to taste them.

Paolo, the son, is waiting to greet us. He runs the small, tasteful hotel off the other side of the courtyard to the kitchen, with the restaurant situated downstairs. He is not expecting us for lunch, but explains that it is no problem, they will find something for us. We stroll along the tree-covered lanes, talk to the dogs, pat the old fat pig, tidy ourselves, and go down for a quick bite.

It soon becomes obvious that it was worth traveling

such a long way on our last day. The seasoned fresh ricotta crepes with puréed wild fennel sauce are light and heavenly and disappear in seconds. Our plates are left gleaming as we madly mop up every last drop of sauce with the just-baked bread.

Next comes a large bowl of rigatoni with a touch of tomato sauce, crushed pepper, fennel, and baby fava beans, finished with a dash of cream. We declare it is the best pasta dish we have sampled on our trip—and we've sampled a lot of pasta. The veal involtini has a rich tomato sauce and is served with a salad of braised bright yellow peppers and potatoes. Lunch ends with fresh cherries from the garden, still on the branches, and a chocolate ricotta tart covered in cocoa.

Robert is eating as though he hasn't been fed for a week. You can always tell when Chef Robert doesn't like the food—he chases it around his plate and moves quickly on to the fresh fruit. No such thing here. He is in his element, and we all comment on how much he's eating. He stops for just a second to say, "This is bloody good food. They can cook!"

We waddle up the stairs to our rooms for a nap. It's hot, so taking off our clothes to sleep is essential, and also allows for "expansion" after such a meal. In 100°F heat, deep in the Sicilian mountains, we sleep for a good hour. Later we sit outside under the trees and reminisce about

the past three weeks. What an adventure it has been. I feel homesick and call my mother, the restaurant, and Beau and Janet (our dog and his babysitter). Funny thing, homesickness. We've been on the move so much I haven't had a chance even to think about it, but the thought of flying out tomorrow brings it flooding over me. I know Robert has been missing his wife, Mary, and his two boys, Gianni and Alessandro. Simon catches the bug and calls home as well. The sun sets, and we go to our rooms to face the ordeal of final packing. I can't bear the thought.

Dinner is another triumph. Wanda cooks, assisted by Giovanna, while Paolo and Peppe, the houseman, run the front of house. They have really captured the essence of eating as you would in someone's home. There are other guests and dinner is served "pronto" at 8:30 p.m. Just as at lunch, there is no menu. Everyone sits at their own table— once again, it is a relief not having to talk to strangers—but we all eat exactly the same food at the same time. Peppe serves us mineral water and delicious local wines, and the feast begins.

First there are deep-fried, pizza-like little breads with fresh tomato sauce. The seasoning of fresh herbs and the intensity of the tomato combined with the crunch of the bread is a great combination.

The meal joyously continues with all our favorites, such as Sicilian spaghetti with mashed sardines and fennel

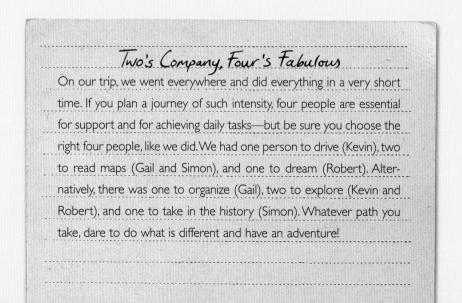

Two's Company, Four's Fabulous

On our trip, we went everywhere and did everything in a very short time. If you plan a journey of such intensity, four people are essential for support and for achieving daily tasks—but be sure you choose the right four people, like we did. We had one person to drive (Kevin), two to read maps (Gail and Simon), and one to dream (Robert). Alternatively, there was one to organize (Gail), two to explore (Kevin and Robert), and one to take in the history (Simon). Whatever path you take, dare to do what is different and have an adventure!

with toasted breadcrumbs sprinkled on top. Again, the seasoning is not shy but gutsy and just right. It's served as the pasta at lunch was, from a huge bowl, and we all take a second helping when it is offered. The bread, again freshly baked, tastes of the wheat it was made with.

Next come big wooden skewers from the grill crammed with sausage, pancetta, and chicken and layered with bay leaves and onions, then dishes of eggplant parmigiana, potato fritters with local pecorino, and finally the Moroccan influence we have searched so hard for in south-western Sicily—heavenly couscous, hand-rolled and saffron-scented. Kevin's happy!

Dessert is home-baked amaretti biscuits covered with vanilla custard, then splashed with a dash each of rum, gin, and Amaretto—what a clever mix of flavors. There's fruit to follow if the guests can possibly open their mouths for more. We do.

When food is cooked from the heart like this, it seems to have a taste like no other. It's not correct to describe it as "simple" cooking, but the food certainly isn't tortured, played with, or put under a technical culinary microscope. It is what it is—a woman and her daughter sharing their fourteenth-century house and their love and knowledge of cooking, which comes from generations of nurturing and respecting traditional recipes and the idea that good food must be part of everyday life.

Nightfall brings fresh mountain air, and our bedrooms have cooled down as we hit the sack for our last sleep in Italy. None of us will fall into a deep sleep tonight; tomorrow we have half of Sicily to drive through before we reach the airport at Catania where we are to catch our plane to Rome. I close my eyes, telling myself: "That's it. No more big meals—just fresh fruit until I get back to Australia."

Gail

Simon and his camera

At the entrance to Tenuta Gangivecchio

The fountain with four faces in the monastery gardens

Braised Peppers with Potato and Crushed Tomatoes

Peperoni al forno

Of the several conquerors of Sicily, the Spaniards are given credit for the introduction of peppers. This delightful braised version, with the addition of potato and tomatoes, can be served as an accompaniment to grilled meats.

Serves 4

1 red pepper
1 yellow pepper
1 green pepper
1 waxy potato (such as Reddale), peeled and finely diced
14 ounces canned, peeled Italian tomatoes with juice
12 basil leaves, torn
⅓ cup olive oil
⅓ cup water
salt
freshly ground black pepper

1. Preheat oven to 400°F. Cut peppers along their natural indentations and remove seeds, inner membranes, and stalk ends.
2. In a heavy casserole dish with a lid, combine all ingredients except salt and pepper. Crush tomatoes gently with the back of a spoon. Season to taste. Bring to a boil, then remove from heat and cover tightly with aluminium foil. Cover with lid.
3. Bake for 30–40 minutes until all ingredients are very soft. Serve warm.

Squash and Ricotta Crepes

Fazzoletti di zucca con ricotta

At Tenuta Gangivecchio this luncheon dish was served with a delicious sauce made from the fennel growing wild around the monastery. Our version adds baked squash.

Serves 4–6

1 cup all-purpose flour
3 eggs
1 cup milk
unsalted butter
salt
1 quantity Tomato Sauce (see page 82)

FILLING
1 pound squash, peeled and cut into chunks
olive oil
salt
freshly ground black pepper
zest of 1 lemon
1 egg
1 pound ricotta

1. Preheat oven to 350°F. Sift flour into a mixing bowl. Make a well and add eggs. Mix gently until shiny; do not overmix. Add milk slowly, stirring until combined. Add ½ cup melted butter and a few pinches of salt. Strain.
2. Melt 3–5 tablespoons of butter in a small pot. Swish a small amount of this butter in a separate, heated 6-inch omelette or crepe pan. Pour excess butter back into small pot.
3. Pour some batter into pan and tilt to deposit a thin, even coat. Cook over medium heat until brown. Turn crepe over and brown other side, then slide onto a plate. Add more butter to pan and repeat process until all batter is used, stacking crepes to cool until filling is ready.
4. To make filling, rub squash chunks with oil, salt, and pepper. Bake until tender and allow to cool. Mash squash with lemon zest, fold in egg and ricotta, and season to taste.
5. To finish dish, lay crepes on work surface and pipe a 1-inch-thick tube of squash mixture along the center of each. Fold one side of crepe over mixture and roll tightly. Grease a cookie sheet well. Cut rolls into 1-inch lengths and arrange cut side up on sheet. Bake for 10–15 minutes. Serve with warmed tomato sauce.

Macaroni with Fava Beans and Pancetta

Pasta con fave

Puréed fava beans have always been considered a food of the poor. We experienced one use of them at Masseria Curatori in Puglia (see recipe on page 63). In this recipe from Tenuta Gangivecchio, the purée is used as a sauce for pasta.

Serves 4

1 quart water
salt
1½ pounds fresh fava beans, shelled
1 large onion, minced
⅓ cup olive oil
4 ounces pancetta, cut into ¼-inch dice
1 cup dry white wine
1 pound good-quality macaroni *or* rigatoni
freshly grated pecorino romano
freshly ground black pepper

1. Bring water to a boil and season liberally with salt. Stir in fava beans and return to a boil. Reduce heat and simmer for 10–15 minutes until very tender. Drain beans and reserve cooking liquid.
2. In a food processor, purée two-thirds of beans until smooth. Reserve remaining beans.
3. In a skillet or frying pan, fry onion in olive oil until golden. Add pancetta and wine and reduce until almost all of the wine has evaporated. Add bean purée and simmer for 5 minutes.
4. Place reserved cooking liquid in a large saucepan and add enough water to make 5 quarts. Add 3 tablespoons salt. Cook pasta until al dente. Drain well, reserving 1 cup of cooking water. Do not rinse pasta.
5. Return pasta to saucepan and add puréed bean sauce and reserved whole beans. Simmer for a few minutes, adding reserved pasta cooking water to thin sauce if required. Serve with pecorino and a few grindings of pepper.

Highlights of the Day

Gail

Kevin

Simon

Robert

Adored Pets

I love people who love animals and the Tornabene family are pet-crazy. Two Siamese cats peered from their balcony along with several canaries and two terriers, with Toto the mutt dog and his beagle friend as outside dwellers. The family has a cemetery just for those precious pets who have departed the monastery.

Family-style Meals

The style of pasta service at Tenuta Gangivecchio was one of the nicest I have ever encountered in a restaurant. We were served from a massive bowl of steaming spaghetti, as if we were in the owners' home. Our Italian "mama" kept returning with the bowl, urging us to eat more.

The Fountain with Four Faces

Water is a precious commodity, especially in the south where the sun is so intense. Did the fountain at the monastery depict four monks spurting acqua dolce or four weary travelers like us, here to rest before continuing on our journey?

Monastery Life

In Sicily, as everywhere in Europe, monks enlightened people in the remotest places. Their religious communities established cultural and economic centers for the locals and introduced farming methods to help develop the area. They were not only teachers but also tenacious workers. The priory at Gangivecchio eventually became a flourishing community.

Wines of Sicily

It is clear that Sicily is poised to break into the forefront of Italian wine production. For many years, paradoxically, it has had more land planted with vines than any other region in Italy. Unfortunately much of the wine produced never gets to the bottle locally, with a large quantity being sold in bulk to the north. Additionally, much of the grape production goes to make sultanas, a key ingredient in many of Sicily's traditional recipes.

Every province of Sicily produces its own signature wines and many of these stay within their own areas. But the tide is turning. With government support, the wine industry is undergoing a transformation. Small wineries are beginning to produce exceptional wines and medium producers are gearing up to break into international markets.

We began our Sicilian sojourn in Taormina under the watchful eye of Mt. Etna. This was the perfect place to sample two selections from Benanti. The Etna Bianco Superiore Pietramarina 1996 is marvelous. It is crisp and dry, with hints of mineral aromas that are typical of great rieslings from Alsace. The Etna Rosso Rovitello 1996 is very stylish with good concentration and balance and a finish of soft, integrated tannins.

To many people, Corvo, made by Duca di Salaparuta, means Sicilian wine. It is Sicily's most famous table wine;

Corvo is actually a brand name. Our introduction to it was the white Corvo Colomba Platino 1998, deceptively easy to drink and with a beautifully smooth freshness. A later tasting of the lesser label, Corvo Glicine 1998, also yielded a white of good fruit and balance.

On the island of Salina we sampled the wines of the Hauner family. Salina Bianco from 1997 and the Rosso from 1996 were very good. But the star of this portfolio is the Malvasia delle Lipari, a dessert wine of beautiful proportion. The grapes are picked late, a week or two after those picked for normal table wines, and then dried on cane mats for fifteen days. The wine exhibits the warmth of the sun with hints of dried ginger and apricots.

Our trip along the northern coast brought us in touch with wines hailing from Palermo and the center of Sicily. From Spadafora, the Don Pietro Rosso 1997 revealed an intense aroma and full rich flavors with ample body. The wines of Tasca d'Almerita were good; in particular, the red and white Regaleali were very dependable. There were two highlights, the Regaleali Rosato being certainly the best rosé in Sicily and the Nozze d'Oro, made from sauvignon blanc, a crisp, zingy wine worth seeking out. The 1996 cabernet sauvignon was less appealing. It is developed, with rich tones of the varietal, but seems disjointed and lacks

harmony. The tannins are characteristically firm, but the wine finishes with an unpleasant stalkiness. Torrevecchia's Casale dei Biscari 1996 yielded a great red wine, intense in its concentration of plum and cherry flavors.

The southwestern leg of our tour brought some delightful surprises. One of Sicily's up-and-coming wineries, Planeta, has burst onto the scene with serious intentions. They produce several traditional varieties, along with today's more popular wines such as cabernet sauvignon, chardonnay, and merlot. La Segreta Bianco and Rosso must be tried, for these are very good wines. The Alastro 1997 is terrific—medium golden with ripe and evolved aromas of green olives and smoky characters. It is an elegant wine, full and with a lovely acid balance to finish. I was less impressed with the Chardonnay 1997. While rich and powerful, it lacks the finesse of the great chardonnays of the world.

Settesoli, near Agrigento, produces Feudo dei Fiori, a blend of chardonnay and inzolia. The 1997 is simply delightful, soft with lemon and vanilla overtones leading to a crisp finish.

One of the most underrated dessert wines of the world is Moscato di Passito di Pantelleria, produced on the tiny island of Pantelleria. Try to find the Martingana from Salvatore Murana. The result is an intriguing wine, delicate yet with concentrated sweetness and a floral character of orange blossoms.

We all loved the wines of Sicily, particularly the traditional varieties. I can only hope that the growth that has occurred to date is further refined and that Sicily concentrates more effort on bringing its wines to the markets that have been underexposed to them.

Kevin

The romantic old monastery in the mountains

A Canon Regular of St. Augustine.

Farewell to Italy

Friday, June 11

We wake up very early, feeling a mixture of excitement to be heading home and sadness that our adventure is at an end. The beginning of the trip seems like a year ago—and yet time has passed like a flash of light and it's hard to believe it's all over.

Simon has rolls and rolls of film that he insists on carrying home by hand. Likewise, Kevin insists on personally carrying a wooden gift box of wines from Marsala, and I refuse to pack the large, beautiful platters we purchased in Taormina and Tropea. Robert has his own thoughts and dreams to ponder. He's been an Italian for three weeks, and his journey into his history has been very different from the frolic around the south that the rest of us have enjoyed.

We meet Giovanna for a quick tour of the monastery before we start our last long drive. She is vibrant, highly motivated, and smart. Part of the upper wing is now a stunning formal dining room, with typically Sicilian views. These mountains are like no other—dry and golden yellow, scattered with rocks, prickly pear, and the occasional olive tree. It's as though they shoot straight up from the ground to tower over us like massive natural skyscrapers.

We walk around the upper stories, where there is a big open fireplace. Giovanna explains how cold the winters here can be and shows us photos of the monastery covered in snow, looking like it's coated in white icing. I'd love to see it, but then I think of trying to get up those perilous roads in such weather. Back in the courtyard, we enter a bank of rooms proposed for a cellar for wine and cheese tasting. The walls are covered with original pastel-colored frescoes of angels, saints, and scenic views of the countryside. This was once the communal eating area for the monks and Giovanna has dreams of turning it into a museum. She is also talking to several people in America who are trying to establish an archaeological scholarship here.

Strolling through the huge legacy the family has inherited, we begin to understand what it means to shoulder responsibility for such a piece of history. Buildings like these constantly demand attention, so the owners need to have a continuous income. They must be enterprising if they are to maintain the place. The Tornabenes have over 125 acres of farmland, but unfortunately it lies idle apart from the existing fruit and olive trees. Income is lost because no one these days wants to work as a laborer on a farm.

We talk a little with Giovanna about where the south has been and where it is going. She says, "It has always been the rich north of Italy and the poor south, with Sicily considered even poorer." In recent years, however, she believes many people have begun to feel that the advent of agritourism in the south, with government backing, has made available a unique product that can be enjoyed by travelers from around the world. If these beginnings are any indication, over the next few years the south should develop a thriving, personal tourism industry. The north, although magnificent with its jewels of Milan, Tuscany, and Venice, is full of tourists. It can only cope, not expand. The north is also cursed with major industry and has a pollution problem that the south will never have. The advantage of industry is constant employment opportunities, but this also means that the majority of migrants to Italy go to the north because that's where the work is. Meanwhile the south stays full of southerners and therefore remains very traditional, except in a couple of seaside towns.

We are captivated by Giovanna's vision of the creation of a unique tourism industry as an enthusiastic way to the future. The south and its produce, cooking, history, and generous people deserve to prosper.

As we drive away from Tenuta Gangivecchio down the mountains, once again we are jammed into the car like sardines in a can. Two hours later we are at Catania, on the east coast. Our worries about crime and theft here disappear as the road takes us directly to the airport without even getting close to the city. We load our bags onto trolleys and drop our dirty, tired Renault back to the rental company, with 2,300 miles on the clock.

For now, the only country on our minds is Australia. Back to our families, our friends, Beau, and Donovans. The adventure, the journey, and the experience are complete. The memories are just beginning.

Gail

Packed and ready for home

An Italian Farewell per Giacomo e Maria (for My Father and Mother)

We drew further and further away from Genoa, our suitcases on the deck behind us packed ready for the new lives awaiting us in Australia. I can still see my mother sobbing, the tears running down her cheeks, clutching my brother and me and waving goodbye to our family on the dock, and my father, his long arms looped around us and his brilliant, brooding coal-black eyes, like the sea at midnight, staring out to the distance, wondering if he will ever see his mother, father, brothers, and sisters again. I can hear him vowing that one day he will bring us back — but sadly, for him and my mother the boat never returned.

Robert

1,2 Fabric for cushions to go on the banquette lounges. 3 Fabric for cane chair seat covers and throw cushions. 4 Fabric for fringed and corded cushions. 5,6,7 Chair covers for the family dining area, introducing citrus colors. 8,9,10 Red-wine, purple, and dark red colors for barstool covers. 11,12,13,14 Fringes and cords for cushions. 15 Fabric for couch covers.

The Inspiration

After three and a half weeks away the restaurant engulfs us as though we've never left, as does Beau. Faced with the day-to-day operation of Donovans and several very tired senior staff, our first month home just flies. Our buoyant mood and the romance of vacationing in Italy fades along with our suntans.

It is our custom at Donovans to change the look and feel of the restaurant every six months, but this summer it will be a much bigger change. We have three months to plan and order all the new decor, put our final plans to the local council for the transformation of the storeroom into a function room, and completely change the menu. It will be like opening for the first time all over again.

We hoped the trip would give us new ideas, and it certainly has. But now each idea has to be converted into a concept and then subjected to a financial analysis to see if we can turn our dreams into reality. We hoped to find beautiful things to eat in Italy—food to inspire and be translated, through Robert's interpretations, onto the plates at Donovans—and ended up experiencing so many exciting dishes that we now need to work out a plan of where to start looking at the menu. We hoped to find beautiful visions for Simon to capture on film. Even though I lived in the south of Italy long ago I didn't remember it to

be so stunningly beautiful. No one has any doubts about the treasures Simon has brought home in his heavy film-laden bag and how persistent he was in his quest to capture the real Sicily. Kevin will start to double the Italian wine list at the restaurant. His detailed documentation of each wine we tasted would make a book in itself.

I have brought back with me the taste of the food and wine, the visions—but most of all I remember the details of the houses and restaurants we visited. The way a cloth was set, a bar, a vase, a stand of old books, rugs, wall hangings—all these things will fit into the annual summer change. Everything will have a touch of Italy. Kevin, Simon, and I start to shop every spare moment and it becomes a ritual for two solid months. We visit all the junk shops, antique stores, Italian groceries, and bookstores we can find. Simon knows the best shops and is instrumental in finding many unusual pieces. Kevin eventually drops out and opts to play golf. It's a fabulous chance for him to play as often as he pleases while I do what I do best—plan, search, and shop.

After eight weeks our spare room at home is full of old baskets, pots and ceramics, wine bottles in woven cane, wooden chairs, benches, trays, bowls and spoons, and all the pottery I couldn't carry home in my luggage. I buy

215

orange- and lemon-shaped plates, terra-cotta wares, and lots of old and cracked things, along with dozens of new cushions, couch covers, chair covers, barstool covers, and curtains in luscious vibrant textures and in the colors of Sicily—hot bold wine colors, Campari colors, lemon, orange, red, pink, yellow, olive green, and citrus. The lounge area will be the heart of all these wild colors, and they will spread gradually to the rest of the restaurant.

Kevin adds a southern Italian selection to our existing wine list, especially Sicilian varieties. As always, we discuss the summer menu with Robert. Usually we sit in a quiet corner of the restaurant with coffee and something sweet and just chat, but this time we have a long, long conversation, reviewing our notes, and sharing thoughts and ideas. Then we leave it all to Robert. A week later he shows us what he is planning. We always love his menus, but this one we adore.

Plans for the new area go to council. The influence is Italian, of course, with food cooked over an open fire. Our commercial exhaust system comes in handy here. The new function room will be called Donovans Kitchen and will be like a typical small restaurant in southern Italy. The guests will sit around a big table and the cook and wait-staff will carve from the rotisserie, chop tomatoes, cook pasta, and serve it to the table right in front of them. It will be natural theater—fresh, wholesome food cooked well and enjoyed with a view of the sea. Actually this area has one of the best seaside views in the restaurant, wasted until now.

By November 1 we are ready to go with the new decor. It takes me and our managers, Darryl and Joseph, from midnight until dawn three nights running to complete the transformation of the restaurant. On the final night everyone is there to help. I'm worried about how much money I've spent and keep thinking Kevin will be furious. However, when every last little detail is put into place no one worries about the cost; we all love it. Simon wants to take photos of it, Robert just strolls around quietly each morning before we open, looking at it—I know that means he likes it—and Kevin, gorgeous as always, is thrilled. I wonder if he really does love it. Sometimes I think he gets his biggest kick from seeing my happiness and pleasure at organizing it all.

The guests that come to Donovans love it too, and in the end, that's really the most important thing. Looking at the way they are eating, drinking, and having fun, I think our changes have worked some magic.

For Kevin, Simon, Robert, and me, the most joyous aspect of the whole experience has been that four very different people with four very different tasks to complete are now better friends than ever. On the trip, despite the pressure of constantly being on the move, things not always going to plan, the incredible heat, and the cramped conditions in the car and in many of the places we stayed, not once did anyone get angry, speak a cross word, leave the group, or not come along on an outing.

I didn't lose my temper or have a fit once—no mean feat for me! Simon lugged his camera everywhere, always looking for the best shots without a word about how sore his shoulders must have been. Robert investigated, tasted, walked, talked to everyone, and gained back the language he thought he might have lost. I fell madly in love all over again with Kevin. His gusto for Italy and the pleasure it gave him, including the driving, made him irresistible to me.

Perhaps the places we went, and what we saw, were too involving to think about petty grievances. Perhaps it's because we knew each other well before we left. Perhaps it's the respect we have for each other and our individual passions. Whatever, it was a joy to start as friends and end our magical time together as even better friends. The bond of the trip and its memories are ours forever.

The only thing to do now is for the four travelers to start planning another journey, to another place, for another dose of inspiration.

Gail

I buy orange- and lemon-shaped plates, terra-cotta wares and
new cushions, couch covers, chair covers, barstool covers and
Sicily — hot bold wine colors, Campari colors, lemon, orange
be the heart of all these wild colors, and they will spread

Lots of old and cracked things, along with dozens of curtains in luscious vibrant textures and in the colors of red, pink, yellow, olive green and citrus. The lounge area will gradually to the rest of the restaurant.

Linguine in the Style of the Fisherman

Linguine con i frutti di mare

This was one of our favorite pasta dish on the trip and has proved to be popular at Donovans too. Its preparation can be tricky because of the timing—the just-cooked pasta must be ready to receive the just-cooked seafood. Choose the best-available ingredients from a quality fishmonger.

Serves 4

5 quarts water
salt
1 pound good-quality linguine
2 cloves garlic, finely sliced
2 bird's-eye chilies, sliced
⅓ cup olive oil
16 black mussels
1 cup chicken stock
4 langoustine (also called Baja lobster)
16 medium shrimp, peeled and deveined, but with tails left on
16 scallops
freshly ground black pepper
handful of Italian parsley, freshly chopped

1. In a large pot, bring water to a boil with 4 tablespoons salt. Cook linguine until al dente.
2. Meanwhile, in a deep skillet or frying pan, fry garlic and chili in olive oil over medium heat; do not brown. Add mussels, which will begin to open within minutes. Discard any that do not open.
3. Increase heat to high and add chicken stock. Reduce by half. (The rapid boiling will create an emulsion between the stock and the olive oil, an essential element in the texture of the finished sauce.)
4. Add langoustines and cook for 1 minute. Add shrimp and cook for 1 minute. Finally, add scallops and cook for 1 minute. Season, but go easy on the salt—mussel juices are already very salty.
5. Drain pasta well but do not rinse. Return to pot and pour seafood and sauce over. Add parsley and toss together. Adjust seasoning.
6. Arrange pasta and seafood with careful carelessness in a large bowl and serve immediately.

Fillets of Blue Eye with Spicy Couscous

Cernia cu'u' cus-cus

Couscous is a gift of the Arabs to Sicilian cuisine and has become a solid part of Sicily's cooking tradition, particularly on the western part of the island. Sicilian couscous recipes are predominantly made with seafood and are a labor of love and patience. This recipe utilizes the traditional method of preparing couscous.

Serves 4

pinch of powdered saffron
salt
water
1 pound couscous
¼ cup olive oil
8 cups chicken stock
10 bay leaves
1 large lemon
freshly ground black pepper
4 fillets blue-eye cod, 7 ounces each
½ cup sultanas

SPICE MIXTURE
½ red pepper
½ yellow pepper
2 cloves garlic
½-inch piece ginger, peeled
1 bird's-eye chili, seeds removed
½ teaspoon cumin seeds
¼ teaspoon coriander seeds
1 star anise
½ teaspoon mild curry powder
2 pinches mace

1. To make spice mixture, blend peppers, garlic, and ginger to a fine paste in a food processor. In a mortar and pestle, pound chili, cumin seeds, coriander seeds, and star anise to a smooth paste. Combine pastes in a small skillet or frying pan and fry over low heat for 3–4 minutes. Stir in curry powder and mace and set aside.

2. Add saffron and 1 teaspoon salt to ½ cup water. Place couscous in a large bowl and add spiced water, 1 tablespoon at a time, rubbing grains between the palms of your hands until all water is absorbed. Repeat procedure with olive oil until all oil is absorbed, about 20–30 minutes.

3. Place chicken stock in a large pot with 5 bay leaves and bring to a boil. Line a heatproof colander with cheesecloth or muslin and place prepared couscous in it, with remaining bay leaves on top. Fold edges of cloth over to cover couscous. Place colander over boiling stock and steam couscous for 45–50 minutes.

4. While couscous is steaming, preheat oven to 400°F. Slice lemon thinly and blanch in boiling water. Cool and reserve. Season fish well.

5. Transfer couscous to a bowl. Stir in sultanas and spice mixture. Set aside and keep warm.

6. Heat a skillet or frying pan and sear fish, skin side down, for 1 minute. Turn onto flesh side and sear for 1 minute. Place in a baking dish and lay 3 slices of lemon on skin side of each fillet. Bake for 4 minutes.

7. Remove any bones from fillets with tweezers and allow fish to rest for 1–2 minutes. Divide couscous between 4 plates and place fish on top. Garnish with roasted peppers (see page 62), if desired. Serve immediately.

Tagliatelle with Tomato, Porcini Mushrooms, Pancetta, and Crumbled Ricotta

Tagliatelle con pomodoro, porcini, pancetta e ricotta

Upon returning home, memories of the mountains of porcini mushrooms at Campo de' Fiori kept flooding back to us. For this recipe we use dried porcini mushrooms; the liquid used to reconstitute them adds a deeper flavor to the sauce.

3½ ounces dried porcini mushrooms, sliced
water
1 medium onion, minced
⅓ cup olive oil
7 ounces pancetta, diced
28 ounces canned, seeded tomatoes with juice, crushed
salt
freshly ground black pepper
1 pound good-quality tagliatelle
8 ounces ricotta

1. Soak porcini mushrooms in ⅓ cup water for 30 minutes.
2. In a deep skillet or frying pan, fry onion in olive oil over low heat until translucent. Add pancetta and cook for 10 minutes to remove fat from meat.
3. Increase heat to medium-high and add porcini mushrooms and their soaking liquid. Reduce by half.
4. Add tomatoes and simmer for 15–20 minutes until mixture thickens slightly. Season with salt and plenty of pepper. Set aside and keep warm.
5. In a large pot, bring 5 quarts water to a boil with 4 tablespoons salt. Cook tagliatelle until al dente. Drain well but do not rinse.
6. Return tagliatelle to pot and add sauce. Stir well so that sauce coats pasta. Adjust seasoning. Serve in warm bowls with ricotta crumbled over each bowl.

Blood Orange Sorbet

Sorbetto di arancia sanguigna

Sicily's second-most important crop, after wheat, is citrus fruit. When you taste a real blood orange such as is grown in Sicily, you will never forget its flavor—it has a rich orange taste with overtones of fresh berries.

Makes approximately 1 quart

2 cups water
2 cups sugar
zest of 2 blood oranges
2 cups blood orange juice

1. In a saucepan, combine water, sugar, and zest. Bring to a boil and boil for 1 minute. Remove from heat. Cool.
2. Stir in blood orange juice and churn in an ice-cream machine according to the manufacturer's instructions.

Our loyal staff at Donovans

Contacts

Accommodation

Hotel Locarno
Via della Penna, 22
00186 Rome
Phone: 39-06/361 0841
Fax: 39-06/321 5249
E-mail: locarno@italyhotel.com

Patria Palace Hotel
Piazzetta Riccardi, 13
73100 Lecce
Phone: 39-0832/245 111
Fax: 39-0832/245 002

Masseria Lo Prieno
Contrada Orelle
73044 Galatone
Phone: 39-0833/861 391
Fax: 39-0833/282 859

Masseria Curatori (Contento family)
Contrada Cristo delle Zolle, 226/227
70043 Monopoli
Phone: 39-080/777 472

Villa Cheta Elite
Via Timpone, 24
85041 Acquafredda di Maratea
Phone: 39-0973/878 134
Fax: 39-0973/878 135

Residence Hotel Le Roccette Mare
Via Mare Piccolo
88038 Tropea
Phone: 39-0963/61 358
Fax: 39-0963/61 450

San Domenico Palace Hotel
Piazza San Domenico, 5
98039 Taormina
Phone: 39-0942/23 701
Fax: 39-0942/625 506

Villa Schuler
Piazzetta Bastione, Via Roma 2
98039 Taormina
Phone: 39-0942/23 481
Fax: 39-0942/23 522
E-mail: hotelschuler@italyhotel.com

Pensione Mamma Santina
Via Sanità, 40
98050 Santa Maria di Salina
Phone: 39-090/984 3054
Fax: 39-090/984 3051

Casa Migliaca
Contrada Migliaca
98070 Pettineo
Phone/Fax: 39-0921/336 722
E-mail: migliaca@mcsystem.it

Grand Hotel Et Des Palmes
Via Roma, 398
90139 Palermo
Phone: 39-091/583 933
Fax: 39-091/331 545

Pensione Tranchina
Via A. Diaz, 7
91014 Scopello
Phone/Fax: 39-0924/541 099

Villa Ravida
Via Roma, 173
92013 Menfi
Phone: 39-0925/71 109
Fax: 39-0925/71 180
E-mail: ravidasrl@iol.it

Villa Athena
Località Panoram. dei Templi, 35
92100 Agrigento
Phone: 39-0922/596 288
Fax: 39-0922/402 180

Tenuta Gangivecchio
Contrada Gangivecchio
90024 Gangi
Phone/Fax: 39-0921/689 191

Restaurants and Cafes

ROME

Trattoria Armando al Pantheon
Salita dei Crescenzi, 31 (a side street just to
the right of the Pantheon)
Phone: 39-06/6880 3034

Ristorante Piperno
Via Monte de' Cenci, 9
Phone: 39-06/6880 6629

Caffè Dolce Vita
Piazza Navona, 70a

Enoteca Cul de Sac
Piazza Pasquino, 73

Trattoria La Torricella
Via E. Torricelli, 2/4
Testaccio
Phone: 39-06/574 6311

LECCE

Caffè Alvino
Piazza Sant'Oronzo, 30

Ristorante Alle Due Corti

OTRANTO

Gelateria Artigianale
Corso Garibaldi, 18
Centro Storico

Ristorante Da Sergio
Corso Garibaldi, 9
Centro Storico
Phone: 39-0836/801 408

MARTINA FRANCA

Trattoria La Cantina
Vico I Lanucara 12
Phone: 39-080/480 8031

TROPEA

Trattoria Vecchia Tropea
Largo Barone

TAORMINA
St Honor (cakes and coffee)
Corso Umberto I, 208

La Gelateria
Corso Umberto I, 135

Ristorante Al Duomo
Piazza del Duomo
Phone: 39-0942/625 656

Ristorante Da Lorenzo
Via Roma, 12
Phone: 39-0942/23 480

NEAR TAORMINA
Grando Albergo Capo Taormina
Via Nazionale, 105
Phone: 39-0942/572 111

Ristorante Da Nino
Via L. Rizzo, 29
Letojanni

PALERMO
Trattoria Shanghai
Vicolo dei Mezzani, 34

AGRIGENTO
Le Caprice Restaurant
Via Panoramica dei Templi, 25
Phone: 39-0922/26 469

Shopping
CLOTHES AND SHOES
Armani Jeans (jeans and casual clothes)
Via del Babuino 70a, Rome

Brandy Menswear
Via dei Giubbonari 40, Rome

The Fans (for soccer fans)
Via Merulana 262, Rome

Blue Store Trend (casual clothes and shoes)
Corso Italia 36, Martina Franca

Antonio Palazzo (eyewear)
Via Vittoria Emmanuele 85, Martina Franca

Paris
Corso Umberto I, Taormina

Scandura Calgature (shoes)
Corso Umberto I 182, Taormina

WINE AND FOOD
Buccone (wine)
Via di Ripetta 19/20, Rome

L'Antica Norcineria (meats and smallgoods)
Campo de' Fiori market, Rome

L'Antica Norcineria (hand-carved prosciutto)
Via della Scrofa 100/100A, Rome

Il Forno di Campo de' Fiori (Rome's best bakery)
Campo de' Fiori 22, Rome

Giuseppe Marazia (terrific cheese)
Piazza Mazzini 50, Lecce

Enoteca Internazionale (good local wine)
Via Cesare Battisti 23, Lecce

Enoteca Massafra Daniele (wine)
Largo d'Aragona, Otranto

Macelleria Rosticceria (butcher)
Via Cavour 19, Martina Franca

Pastaficio Conti (fresh pasta)
Via Oronzo Dellita, Martina Franca

Tropea's Alimentari
Enogastronomia
Via Regina Margherita, Tropea

Delize de Calabria
Via Indipenza, Tropea

Prodotti Casarecci
Largo Vaccari, Tropea

La Torinese (wine and food)
Corso Umberto I 59, Taormina

Carlo Hauner winery
Via Umberto I Loc. Lingua, Santa Maria di Salina
Phone/Fax: 39-090/984 3141

Antica Focacceria San Francesco
Via A. Paternostro 58, Palermo

Cantine Florio (Marsala wine)
Via Vincenzo Florio 1, Marsala
Phone: 39-0923/781 111
Fax: 39-0923/982 380

HOMEWARES
In Lecce – Dolce & Gabbana, Mandarin Duck, Frette (linen)

Piccoli Pensieri di Carecci Cosoma (pottery)
Corso Garibaldi, Centro Storico, Otranto

La Colori di Caes (bed linen)
Via Frieste 6, Martina Franca

La Vecchia Forgia (pottery and ceramics)
Via Umberto I, Tropea

Trionfante Antichita (antiques and collectables)
Corso Umberto I 170–172, Taormina

Narise (perfume and soap)
Corso Umberto I 33, Taormina

S-And (inexpensive, good-quality linen)
Corso Umberto I 88, Taormina

Ceramiche Art Souvenirs
Via Teatro Greco 7, Taormina

Index